W9-AGV-709

SUICIDE CLUSTERS

SUICIDE CLUSTERS

Loren Coleman

Faber and Faber, Inc.
Boston London

 Published in the United States by Faber & Faber, Inc., 50 Cross Street, Winchester, Massachusetts 01890.

Library of Congress Cataloging-in-Publication Data

Coleman, Loren.
Suicide clusters.

1. Suicide. 2. Suicide—Prevention. I. Title.
HV6545.C56 1987 362.2 86-29065
ISBN 0-571-12983-8
ISBN 0-571-12991-9 (pbk.)

Dedicated to David P. Phillips,
the author of the Werther effect concept

Table of Contents

Acknowledgments

SEARCHING and exploring the literature of suicide clusters is not an easy task. Locating the kinds of records I desired often meant tracking down some obsure journal, or book, hidden away someplace, dusty and long forgotten. Other times it meant contacting and interviewing people who had lost someone close to them, or deeply investigating a series of suicides. Because of this dimension of the work, a book such as *Suicide Clusters* is, of course, really the combined efforts of years of many people's labor. I gratefully acknowledge the toil of all the researchers, sociologists, psychologists, suicidologists, anthropologists, social workers, police, parents, doctors, librarians, teachers, and others who had the tidbits of evidence I sought, and was able to discover. Any oversights I have made in not giving due credit to a specific person, within the text or my detailed bibliography, must remain mine.

While this book was being developed and created, several people were important in terms of their support and intellectual stimulation. As always, probably the first people to suffer in an author's life are those in his family. This book, while emotionally draining and creatively exciting, did place me in that never-neverland of writing, and I affectionately thank Libbet and Malcolm for tolerating my periods of deep involvement in this work. Their support, was critical. Libbet, furthermore, is my best first reader, and I appreciate her useful insights. Malcolm kept me in touch with the love and reality of his youthful wants and my strong parenting needs.

Bibliographically speaking, the following individuals contributed helpful items or ideas that became the bricks and mortar of the book: Alan Berman, Cathy Baron, Charles Henegar, Daniel Cohen, David Phillips, George Eberhart, Helaine Hornby, Janet Brysh, John Keel, Joseph Zarzynski, Lynn Bratman, Madelyn Gould, Mark A. Hall, Michael Hoffman, Patrick Huyghe, Richard Melito, Robert Rickard, Sherry Baker, Shinichiro Namiki, Wanda Berry, and William Porter. Sally Brown was involved in a detailed review of the work, and I thank her for helpful comments. Marsha Stultz assisted in the search into past incidents, the chronological listing, and likewise gave the book a critical reading in its draft stages. I would not have finished this book without them.

As always, I wish to thank the fine folks at Faber and Faber, past and present, namely Doug Hardy, Susan Nash, Vicki Rosenberg, Stephen Williamson, Tom Kelleher, Betsy Uhrig, and Nancy Dutting, who reinforced my images of this project, and saw it through to publication.

Finally, I was supported, in various ways, by my colleagues at the Human Services Development Institute, Center for Research and Advanced Study, University of Southern Maine, and the Department of Sociology and Anthropology, University of New Hampshire. Of those at the latter, I especially would like to acknowledge Gerri King and Peggy Plass for some friendly intellectual and temporal support, as well as Karl Pillemer, Murray Straus, and Kirk Williams for some theoretical ideas.

My hope is that the evidence I have collected for *Suicide Clusters* will assist in the future research into the mysteries of the phenomenon, and help in tomorrow's preventive efforts.

LOREN COLEMAN
Portland, Maine
January 1987

Introduction

EVERY NINETY minutes one teenager in the United States will take his or her own life, while every nine minutes a teenager will make an attempt to kill himself or herself. The numbers are staggering and difficult to absorb. This week more than 125 adolescents will commit suicide and one thousand others will try. This year perhaps as many as seven thousand young people will end their own lives. In the last two decades, the suicide rate among American teens has jumped by three hundred percent.

Nationally, suicide is the third leading cause of death among adolescents; in some cases, the number one and two killers, accidents and homicides, are viewed by many researchers as disguised suicides. Many drug overdoses, fatal automobile accidents, and related self-destructive eating and alcoholic disorders are uncounted teen suicides. Some researchers feel that because some suicides are hidden, unreported, or masked as one-car automobile accidents, for example, the total really may be more like twenty-five thousand young people a year. In some states, such as Nevada and Maine, suicide is the second leading cause of death for teens. Many young people view suicide as an acceptable alternative to their problems.

More girls than boys will attempt suicide, but more boys will complete the act.

Such statistics have convinced many that teen suicides are epidemic in America. Congress held hearings on the pervasive nature of the problem in October 1984, and the national media focused on the issue by way of documentaries, made-for-television movies, and news specials throughout the mid-1980s. Indeed, according to some media commentaries, the "featured crisis" for the 1985 television season was teen suicides. The trend continued in 1986, with the rebroadcast of some of these movies, and the screening of new afternoon specials and features.

In the midst of this apparent wave of youth suicides, something strange started happening, or, at least, was noticed for the first time by a wide spectrum of the public. In little pockets around the country—Plano, Texas, February 1983; Westchester County, New York, February 1984; and Omaha, Nebraska, February 1986—clumps of adolescent suicides began appearing. These suicide clusters were little understood, and seemed a new and more menacing threat to the future of our youth.

What exactly is a suicide cluster? Suicide-prevention and public health officials during the early 1980s were confused by the extent and nature of the problem, and unsure in their attempts to explain what was going on. No one really had all the answers. No one knew even how to define the problem.

In this book, the notion of suicide clusters will be explored. As with any concept that has gone largely underexamined, this investigation is a beginning, a launching place from which to start other examinations. First, for the sake of a common point of reference, let us look at some commonly agreed upon ideas on suicide and its science, suicidology.

Emile Durkheim, who appears to be an early skeptic of suicide clusters, wrote the bible on the subject of suicide in 1897. In his *Suicide,* he formulated three types of suicide: altruistic, anomic, and egoistic. Briefly, according to *A Modern Dictionary of Sociology,* altruistic is "a type of suicide in which an individual who is very closely integrated into a group or society kills himself for the welfare of the group." Anomic is "a type of suicide that results from normlessness or social and personal disorganization." Egoistic is "suicide that is due to the existence of strong social norms for which the individual is made to feel personally responsible, resulting in an overwhelming burden on the individual."

While these differences are extremely important in understanding the possible motivations behind completed suicides, for our purposes, the central theme we are pursuing is the mechanism and contagion among individuals which spreads the suicidal behavior. For example, while the suicides of the Jewish defenders of Masada are often labeled altruistic and seem very unlike the suicides chronicled below of Greek virgins or today's teens, our belief is that there may be a similar underlying process that links the chains of suicides, no matter what their types. This mechanism is contagion, and the concept has been popularly captured by the use of the phrase *suicide clusters.*

Individuals commit suicide frequently because they feel isolated, neglected, and unheard by other members of society. Often ostracism from a group can cause an unbearable pain, leading to suicide. Paradoxically, suicide clusters demonstrate a linkage between individuals, a true group or collective behavior beyond the society's norms.

Suicide is seen by many people, and especially teens, as the solution to a seemingly overwhelming deluge of problems. Severe behavioral conflicts, depression, loss of a loved one (from a parent to a pet), failures at school or work, confusion over sex roles, substance abuse, and a long list of other so-called "risk factors" can push them over the edge, and start them thinking about suicide as an attractive alternative to their present state of affairs.

As the Centers for Disease Control pointed out in its 1986 publication, *Youth Suicide in the United States, 1970–1980,* one of the most under-researched risk factors may be "exposures to suicides" in one's social network. As the report notes, direct exposure for teens may be a classmate's or friend's suicide, and indirect exposure may occur through news reports, movies, books, or discussions. We will present accounts that document that these types of exposure do influence future suicides and create suicide clusters.

Suicide clusters. The words convey such a frightening, yet mysterious feeling. The word *suicide,* which came into use around 1651, simply and tragically, is the act of killing oneself. *Cluster,* appearing about 110 years before *suicide,* means a collection of things of the same kind found close together, a group, swarm, crowd. When the two words are placed together, as happened during the 1980s series of teen suicide clusters in the United States, people had only a foggy idea of what was meant. The words referred, in an elementary way, to a number of suicides close together. But what number? And close together how?

Mark Rosenberg, chief of the Violence Epidemiology Division at the Centers for Disease Control, was one of the first researchers to define the term, *suicide clusters*. Speaking at the National Conference on Youth Suicide in 1985, he said they were groups of deaths, closely related in time and space, having at least three or more completed suicides. Usually, they were suicides of young white males. Are clusters merely coincidence? Rosenberg did not think so, and felt there was a definite association among the adolescent suicides occurring within a short period of time in the same locale. Later, speaking about the February 1986 cluster in Omaha, Rosenberg said that one suicide "may be a model" for others in the community who had been "at risk" of doing the same thing. In August 1986, Rosenberg compared suicide to a contagious disease, and believed it could spread quickly. "You have to wonder if exposure to a first suicide triggers the later deaths in these kinds of clusters," he said.

The uses, and thus the definitions of the words in context, have varied. In some recent examinations of groups of adolescent suicides, the time period has been anywhere from a weekend to two years. Some collections of suicides have numbered over a dozen, others more, but in spite of Rosenberg and others who feel clusters must be a collection of three or more suicides, in some cases the media have labeled an event a suicide cluster when it involved only one *completed* (suicidologists have rejected the word *successful*) suicide and several attempts. Geographically speaking, often the suicides have been committed by individuals in the same school, town, or county. But other seemingly related clusters, as in southeastern New York in 1984, covered three large metropolitan counties. Other clusters have encompassed whole countries or groups of nations.

In the psychiatric literature, the word *cluster* was at first linked to suicidal attempts. In past suicidological works, several different words have been used for what today might be termed a suicide cluster. *Suicide epidemic*, for example, has often been defined as a series of suicides moving like a contagious disease through a community, area, or country. Other old records talk of "waves of suicides" in much the same way we discuss suicide clusters. A supposedly specific form of suicide labeled *mass suicide* is frequently felt to mean only a large number of suicides, often altruistic, committed all at the same time in exactly the same setting. While that sometimes is the case, as in the Jonestown, Guyana, mass suicide of 1978, the words have also been used in a broader sense, as with mass suicide researcher Joseph A.M. Meerloo's statements regarding the suicides of Jewish and non-Jewish residents of Nazi Germany.

In this book, the terms *cluster suicide, suicide epidemic, waves of suicides*, and *mass suicide* all are seen as merely different variations on the same theme, suicide clusters. Some of these words seem frozen in a temporal or cultural context by various writers, but for our purposes, there seems little difference between five suicides in five months, or five thousand in five minutes. Further refinement of the concept shall naturally follow the data in future works, but the problem we have discovered is that no one has collected the totality of the clustering events, or conducted a review of the suicide clusters throughout time and beyond the borders of America. This work will do just that, so future sociologists, suicidologists, parents, school officals, and the general public who must confront this problem will know what has happened in the past. As George Santayana said in a frequently quoted passage, "Those who cannot remember the past are condemned to repeat it." It seems that some people have written about suicide clusters as if they are just a phenomenon of adolescents in the 1980s, and this study will explore thoroughly some recent teen clusters. Additionally, this work will demonstrate that suicide clusters appear among diverse age groups. Others have mentioned the suicides of six University of California at Berkeley students in 1966 as the first suicide cluster in history. This book should put that notion to rest as well.

One last note: the discussing of suicide is often like talking about baseball. Baseball can be viewed in terms of statistics or stories. Baseball fans tend to be divided between those who love the stats and those who love to read, for example, about Babe Ruth's career. Both are important, and the same is true of suicide studies. The statistics on suicides are overwhelming and scary, but the human pain after the death of a loved one lies on another level. The impact of suicides cannot be felt deeply by a book of pure suicide statistics. For that reason, the work you are about to read delves into the real stories of real people's lives and deaths. Some of these accounts were painful to research and painful to write about. But to understand the problem, to completely explore its ramifications, the full details of many of these suicides are revealed here. Perhaps through a look at the narrative information, we all may begin to discover the hidden messages in some of these acts and search for ways to prevent future suicide clusters.

Part 1

"It is fear that first brought gods into the world."
—Petronius,
first century A.D.

In Search of Ancient Clusters

The Greeks

ONE OF THE first documented suicide clusters occurred during the fourth century B.C., in Miletus, the mother city of Euxine. Just as Jason, Hercules, and the other Argonauts explored the Euxine for the metaphorical answer to their global questions about the meaning of life by way of "the golden fleece," this too is where our search for insights into the phenomenon of an unexplored form of suicide shall begin.

Miletus, decidedly the greatest Greek city before 500 B.C., occupied a very favorable place at the end of the rich valley of Asia Minor's Maeander River, was a natural outlet for trade, and so all matter of folk traveled through this city. Its four harbors were world renowned, and its influence extended far inland, as well as east across the Black Sea, and south to Egypt. The whole region was so astir with Greek enterprise that the Greeks came to regard this quarter of the world, once looked upon as remote and inhospitable, as almost a part of the home country.

Miletus was the seat of great literary and religious activities. Thales, Anaximander, Anaximenes, and Hecataeus all lived and wrote in Miletus. One place they certainly visited was the chief temple of the city, on the southeastern side, that of Apollo Delphinius.

The record of this early suicide cluster comes down to us by way of the writings of Plutarch, the Greek biographer, historian, and writer. His accounts on the cluster of Miletus were written many years after the incidents there, but his authority on the matter is deeply respected. Later scholars, from the context of the accounts, date the Miletus cluster from some time between 400 and 301 B.C. According to Plutarch:

> *A strange and terrible affliction came upon the maidens of Milethos, from some obscure cause—mostly it was conjectured that some poisonous and ecstatic temperament of the atmosphere produced in them a mental upset and frenzy. For there fell suddenly upon all of them a desire for death and a mad impulse towards hanging. Many hanged themselves before they could be prevented. The words and the tears of their parents, the persuasions of their friends, had no effect. In spite of all the ingenuity and cleverness of those who watched them, they succeeded in making away with themselves. The plague seemed to be of an unearthly character and beyond human remedy, until on the motion of a wise man a resolution was proposed that women who hanged themselves should be carried out to burial through the market-place. The ratification of this resolution not only checked the evil but altogether put an end to the passion for death. A great evidence of the high character and virtue of the women was this shrinking from dishonour and the fact that they who were fearless in face of the two most awful things in the world—death and pain—could not support the appearance of disgrace nor bear the thought of shame after death.*

In another comment on this cluster, Plutarch noted that the decree stated the virgins were to be carried naked through the marketplace, and "the passage of this law not only inhibited but quashed their desire of killing themselves." Why would Greek virgins begin to kill themselves in such great numbers that it would be noted as extraordinary? Mass suicide researcher Joseph Meerloo described these suicides as a "mass epidemic of the satyr delusion occuring in Miletus. Young girls began to indulge in all kinds of ecstatic and orgiastic bodily movements which eventually led to epileptic convulsions and suicide."

Perhaps Miletus was the site of more than one wave of suicides among its young women, for from the third century B.C., we find Tegea recording this epitaph from a gravestone: "We leave you, Miletus, dear homeland, because we refused unlawful sex to impious Gauls. We were three maidens, your citizens. Violent war with the Celts brought us to this fate. We did not wait for unholy union or marriage, but we found ourselves a protector in Death."

Another Greek location, Leucadia, was famous for its suicides in pagan times during the fourth and fifth centuries B.C. At the extreme southwest end of that island stood a temple to Apollo on a broken white cliff. Near it existed a regular spot for lover-suicides, on which account it was named Lover's Leap. From this promontory, according to what records we have, a series of notables committed suicide, including the poet Sappho of Lesbos and Queen Artemisia of Caria, ending their pangs of unrequited love and sorrow by jumping into the sea. These suicides were often witnessed by large crowds, and later celebrated in poetry and history.

A common theme running through these early Greek suicide clusters was that of passion, intimacy, and sexual feelings. Interestingly, if we look closely at the Greek mythic character Pan, we discover a personification of some of the feelings hidden beneath the surface of these suicides. Pan, the goat-footed, manlike god, was supposed to preside over shepherds and flocks, and to delight in rural music. He was the giver of fertility, and thus he was shown as phallic, vigorous, and lustful. Representations of Pan often show him frolicking with virgins in the hillsides.

Pan, however, was also regarded as the creator of sudden and groundless terror, *panic*. The word *panic*, which appeared in English about A.D. 1600, symbolized the contagious emotion that was attributed to the influence of Pan, a sudden and excessive feeling of alarm or fear, usually leading to extravagant or injudicious efforts to secure safety. Literally, Pan made humans stampede in terror. As you will see from the cases of suicide waves that unfold in this book, the combined elements of satyrism (with its essential component of companionship and/or loss of it) and panic are two important underlying parts of clusters.

The connection among some of history's group virgin-suicides, satyrism, the myth of Pan, panic, and other suicide clusters may have been noticed by the Greeks long ago, but was apparently forgotten in later, more repressive times. In Pan, and through his effect—panic—we see the personification of behavioral contagion, the spreading of one form of conduct or action from person to person. This is the element linking all the stories you are about to read.

The Romans

Records of clusters in the early days of the Roman Empire have also been found. Many of the soldiers who had fought under Tarquin the Proud, circa 600 B.C., were forced to work in the sewers of Rome, and because of this distasteful labor, soon took to killing themselves. This suicide epidemic was stopped by Tarquin, however, when he ordered the body of every suicide be nailed to a cross and publicly exposed.

The poet Horace, who lived from 65 B.C. to 8 B.C., noted in his day that many suicides were occurring from the Fabrician Bridge into the Tiber River. His view of suicide gives some insight into its place during his time. His most famous quotation is: "He who saves a man against his will as good as murders him."

During the first century B.C., Pliny the Elder expressed a similar notion when he wrote: "Amid the sufferings of life on earth, suicide is God's best gift to man."

During the reign of Claudius I, A.D. 41 to A.D. 54, quite a few men took their own lives. Seneca the Younger, famed Roman rhetorician, who was later also to commit suicide in A.D. 65, wrote Lucilius, and told of the many people of all ages and ranks who were killing themselves. He further observed that the epidemic had reached even circus performers, at the time regarded on a par with Roman civil war heroes.

The Vikings

In the antiquity of the Norsemen there are hints of groupings of suicides. The Viking concept of death existing as a concrete and positive place to go speaks to the reasoning behind some suicide clusters. Valhalla, the abode of Odin in Asgard, was seen as a warrior's paradise to which only those who died violently could go. The roof of Valhalla was made of polished shields upheld by spears.

Troops of heroes issued daily from its 540 doors to delight themselves in battle, and return to drink and feast and hear tales into the night. Valkyries, Odin's beautiful handmaidens, served at the banquets, but were best known as the "choosers of the slain," being sent forth by Odin to every battle, and to every suicide location. They ride through the air, and with their spears designate who shall die, afterward conducting the slain back to Valhalla. In Sweden, where death and a trip to Valhalla were highly regarded, people frequently flung themselves from lofty rocks rather than die in some other more mundane fashion. Several of these rocks in Sweden are termed *allestenar*, or "family rocks." One is located on the shore of a lake in Bleking province. Two found in West Gotland are named Valhal, because they supposedly stand at the entrance of Valhalla. For our purposes, perhaps most interesting is another of these rocks, named Stafva Hall, which by tradition was the location in ancient times of wholesale suicides by Odin's worshipers.

In Iceland, one such rock exists from which many "afflicted and unhappy ones" committed suicide by leaping to "depart unto Odin." Anthropologist Paul H. Mallet, in his 1873 book, *Northern Antiquities*, quotes an ancient saga: "It is useless to give ourselves up to groans and complaints, or to put our relations to needless expenses, since we can easily follow the example of our fathers, who have all gone by the way of this rock."

The Norsemen's, like many of today's, suicide clusters were enhanced by a specific and positive view of death. The elaborate Viking mythology, concerning the location a victim would travel to after a leap from the rocks, made suicide a good second choice if one could not die in battle. In a parallel fashion, modern suicidologists have discovered that a twentieth-century teenager's concept of death is often filled with complex myths about how the teen will be able to come to his or her own funeral, watch the parents' and friends' reactions, and spend death in a pleasant, wondrous paradise. Death imagined in such terms has apparently led to suicide clusters.

The Jewish Legacy

One mass suicide in Jewish history is well known, that of the 960 defenders of Masada in A.D. 73. But few realize that many other suicide clusters are to be found in the chronicles of Flavius Josephus from the time of the Jewish-Roman conflicts.

Josephus wrote that in 63 B.C. when Jerusalem fell to Pompey "countless numbers" of citizens burnt their homes and jumped from cliffs. In 20 B.C., after an unsuccessful revolt against Herod, the Gadarens killed themselves *en masse* by sword in their homes, or by jumping from cliffs and drowning in rivers.

Josephus noted that in A.D. 67 the army of Vespasian, after a forty-seven-day siege, overran the citizens of Jotapata, and seeing "they could kill none of the Romans, they resolved to prevent being killed by the Romans, and got together in great numbers, in the utmost parts of the city, and killed themselves." Indeed, Josephus had been deeply involved in one of the first mass suicides to be recorded, that of thirty-nine eminent men of Jotapata holed up in a cave with Josephus. After the Romans discovered the cave, Josephus and the men discussed a suicide pact as an alternative to capture. The Jotapata citizens were determined, despite Josephus's pleas. Finally they drew lots, and Josephus and another were scheduled to be last. Josephus talked the other man out of the plan, they surrendered to the Romans, and Josephus began his career as an adviser and friend of the Romans.

Other mass suicides, according to Josephus, occurring in A.D. 67, were some Jotapata soldiers who killed themselves by sword rather than surrender to the Romans, and a group of Joppa sailors who decided to die also by sword instead of drowning when their ship began to sink in a storm. In an incident that may be the largest mass suicide event in history, Josephus detailed the army of Vespasian's siege of Gamala, near Mount Tabor. As the end was at hand, many Gamalans retreated to the city's citadel. Then, in Josephus's words:

> *The Romans got up and surrounded them, and some they slew before they could defend themselves, and others as they were delivering up themselves; and the remembrance of those that were slain at their former entrance into the city increased their rage against them now; a great number also of those that were surrounded on every side, and despaired of escaping, threw their children and their wives, and themselves also, down the precipices, into the valley beneath, which, near the citadel, had been dug hollow to a vast depth . . . while the Romans slew but four thousand, whereas the number of those that had thrown themselves down was found to be five thousand.*

That five thousand died in this mass suicide incident has not been disputed by such suicidologists as Dr. L.D. Hankoff, who examined the event in his article on suicides in Jewish history. We can only ponder why more has not been written on the Gamalans' deaths. One clue, of course, is that the source of this account, Josephus's *Wars of the Jews*, Book IV, Chapter 1, is a relatively short passage, compared to the space he and others since have devoted to Masada. Furthermore, as Hankoff points out in his article on the matter, Josephus "allows the most admiration for the Masada defenders."

Masada is the most famous mass suicide of ancient times. In A.D. 73, with the Romans winning battle after battle in their war in Judea, the last Jewish stronghold was the mountaintop fortress founded by the Maccabees and made nearly impregnable by Herod the Great. Masada played a great part during the war, holding out for some time after the fall of Jerusalem. In the end, however, the defenders of the huge rocky mesa three hundred yards wide, six hundred yards long, and a sheer twelve hundred feet above the Dead Sea found themselves in a hopeless battle against the Roman Tenth Legion's fifteen thousand soldiers. As the siege of Masada was coming to a close, the Jews' commander and leader, Eleazar Ban-Yair, gave a lengthy speech persuading his followers, consisting of nearly a thousand Zealots, to set an "example which shall at once cause their astonishment at our death, and their admiration of our hardiness therein." When Masada had to surrender its garrison, the men first killed their wives and children, then themselves. As the Romans made their final assault, they were greeted by a "terrible solitude on every side" and "a perfect silence" but no enemy. Instead, they found 960 dead men, women, and children of Masada.

Early Christians

The impact of the early Christian church was great, for the dramatic deaths of the first Christian leaders often profoundly influenced the mass reactions taken by their followers. Martyrs of early Christianity sometimes sparked clusters of suicides that followed in their wake. When St. Ignatius of Antioch, in about A.D. 107 or 116 (authors disagree on the proper year), was led to the Roman amphitheater, he requested of his captors the right to secure his crown of martyrdom. He stated that, if necessary, he would himself provoke the wild beasts to kill him. "I bid all men know that of my own free will I die for God, unless ye shall hinder me. . . . Let me be given to the wild beasts. . . . Entice the wild beasts that they become my sepulchre . . . come fire and cross and grapplings with wild beasts, wrenching of bones, hacking of limbs, crushings of my whole body; only be it mine to attain unto Jesus Christ."

As suicide researcher James O'Dea noted, "the contagion of this feeling spread to the general body of Christians." Many did provoke wild animals to kill them; others leapt into fires with "exclamations of joy"; still others jumped from their tall homes. St. Perpetua, according to St. Cyprian, helped raise to her throat the trembling right hand of the young gladiator who was to slay her.

Preservation of chastity was the second most frequent reason for suicide, after martyrdom, in the early Christian church. One noteworthy cluster has been related to this form of suicide. When the German Visigoth king Alaric invaded and plundered Rome on the twenty-fourth of August, A.D. 410, many Christian virgins of the city committed suicide to avoid being raped by the conquerors. How many killed themselves is open to debate. Edward Gibbon in his *The Decline and Fall of the Roman Empire* noted:

> *Augustine intimates that some virgins or matrons actually killed themselves to escape violation; and though he admires their spirit, he is obliged, by his theology, to condemn their rash presumption. Perhaps the good bishop of Hippo was too easy in the belief, as well as too rigid in the censure, of this act of female heroism. The twenty maidens (if they ever existed) who threw themselves into the Elbe when Magdeburg was taken by storm, have been multiplied to the number of twelve hundred.*

St. Augustine also discussed an epidemic of suicide among the sect of Donatists, especially the party named the Circumcelliones of North Africa, in the fourth century A.D. They felt they were apostles of death, and thus, would daily try to kill themselves by jumping from rocks, burning themselves alive, or by forcing others to kill them. Often they would stop travelers on highways, and through bribes or threats, try to induce these invididuals to kill them. Besides openly courting martyrdom, they did manage to kill themselves in great numbers.

The tradition of suicide clusters among early Christian sects is a long one, and has been carried into more recent times. For example, during the thirteenth century, the Albigenses, a Christian sect living in the south of France, often committed mass suicides through fasting and self-bleeding.

Europeans of the Middle Ages

During the Middle Ages, disease-stricken European lands were often the sites of suicide clusters as a direct result of the pestilence and illness sweeping the population. In seventh-century England a pestilence, probably the bubonic plague, devastated the land, and many people turned to suicide. As one contemporary, Roger of Wendor, wrote: "In the year of Grace 665, there was such an excessive mortality in England, that the people crowded to the seaside, and threw themselves from the cliffs into the sea, choosing rather to be cut off by a speedy death than to die by the lingering torments of the pestilence."

In 1027, 1237, 1278, and 1418, throughout Europe, as epidemics of St. Vitus's dance gripped the people, many committed suicide. Similarly, St. John's dancing mania, beginning on 24 June 1374, caused suicides all over Europe. Sweating sickness, something like influenza with a high fever, turned up in epidemic waves in Europe in 1485, 1517, and 1551; in London in 1506; and in England and Germany in 1528. The horror of the sweating sickness led great numbers of people to take their own lives while attempting to escape their suffering. Between the fifteenth and sixteenth centuries, especially in Italy, due to the Tarantula mania, or tarantism as it is more commonly known today—a dancing mania similar to St. Vitus's—many people were overcome and drowned themselves in the sea.

During these days of darkness, religion was blamed, once again, for a major suicide cluster of women. Pope Gregory VII, between the years 1074 and 1078, issued various decrees imposing celibacy on the clergy of the Catholic Church. Before Gregory VII, priests in the Roman Catholic Church had wives, a little-known fact today. This pope is, indeed, credited with formulating the ideal of the papacy as a structure embracing all peoples, and educating the clergy and lay world in rigid obedience to Rome. What is also little realized is that his decrees against married priests caused a wave of suicides among discarded wives thoughout Europe.

Suicide epidemics among Jews during the Middle Ages were a frequent event, as they were often the target of persecution. In France, in 1095, a large number killed themselves to escape torture. In 1190, anti-Jewish riots broke out in the walled city of York, and the Jews, headed by Josce, were allowed by the sheriff to take refuge in the royal castle. Soon the castle was besieged, and York's Jews were given the choice of renouncing their religion or killing themselves. On 16 and 17 March 1190, from the walls of the castle that still sits on a mound in the middle of York, six hundred Jews committed suicide. Today a simple plaque stands by the castle in their memory.

In 1320, another five hundred Jews came to the same end during the siege of the Castle of Verdun on the Garonne in France. During the Black Death of 1348 to 1350, Jews were accused of poisoning wells throughout Europe, and many burned themselves to death in their synagogues or killed themselves in their homes to avoid the fury of the masses.

The Middle Ages was a time of many group suicides that are only footnotes in the available records, and thus can be mentioned only briefly. These include the suicide clusters of the women in Marseilles and Lyons, the many suicide epidemics during the reign of France's Hugh Capet from A.D. 987 to 996, and the massive suicide waves of many Christian soldiers who put on the mantles of fallen Knights Templar and were martyred after the Battle of Hitten during the Crusades.

New World Slaves

Suicides are a little-known part of the history of slavery in the New World. In the West Indies, during the sixteenth century, many suicide clusters spread through the slaves of Spanish plantation owners. The Indian slaves were killing themselves in such high numbers because of the cruelties inflicted upon them that the population decreased greatly. One proprietor was so upset by the suicide epidemic, he stopped it by threatening to kill himself and follow his slaves with increased severe treatment into the next world.

After the conquest of the New World by the Spanish, mass suicides were frequent in Mexico and Peru due to the hard forced labor in the mines. Faced with despair and persecution, the native peoples of Central and South America turned to suicide. One Yucatan chief who found himself in slavery called together ninety-five of his followers, and observed: "My worthy companions and friends, why desire we to live any longer under so cruel a servitude? Let us now go unto the perpetual seat of our ancestors, for we shall then have rest from these intolerable cares and grievances which we endure under the subjection of the unthankful. Go before; I will presently follow." And so he did, after he gave each one poisonous leaves, which they burnt and inhaled. They all died.

The Russians

Frequent outbreaks of suicide clusters in Russia have been recorded down through the years. For example, historian James O'Dea wrote that during one epidemic in 1666, whole communities were said to have killed themselves during a revival of religious fanaticism. After the Jonestown mass suicide, *Time* magazine noted: "In the 17th century, Russian Orthodox dissenters called the Old Believers refused to accept liturgical reforms. Over a period of years some 20,000 peasants in protest abandoned their fields and burned themselves." While the total number may not be correct, the record speaks of many groups of suicides in Russia.

Certainly, Russia does have a significant history of secret religious sects, some of which have taken suicide as one of their major tenets. Among these, one was the *soshigateli*, or self-burners, who regarded voluntary death by fire as the only means of purification from the sins and pollution of the world. They abounded in Siberia in the 1850s. Between 1855 and 1875, groups of *soshigateli* numbering fifteen to one hundred burned themselves in large pits or solitary buildings filled with brushwood. About the year 1867, seventeen hundred were reported to have voluntarily chosen death by fire near Tumen, in the Eastern Urals. Another sect with similar tendencies, the *morestschiki*, or self-sacrificers, preferred iron to fire. In 1868, a massive mystical sacrifice took place on the Gurieff Estate on the Volga, where forty-seven men and women killed themselves with swords.

A religious suicide cluster occurred in 1897, at Tiraspol, Moldavia, when twenty-eight individuals buried themselves alive to escape a census enumeration that they apparently believed was sinful. A cluster of children's suicides is reported by Lucy Davidson for the years 1908 to 1910 in Moscow.

Islands of Clusters

NOT ALL SUICIDE clusters have occurred in the distant past. Waves of self-destructive behavior have continued during the modern era. More recent teen suicide clusters will be reviewed in Part Two, but here some reports infrequently noted elsewhere will be surveyed. In this chapter we shall explore the geographic context that connects these islands of clusters.

Japan and Saipan

Japan has long been associated in the Western mind with suicide. The nation's tradition of *hari-kari* and *seppuku* (ritual suicides) are well known, and the mass suicides of its warriors are excellently documented. Five thousand young airmen, for example, died in kamikaze missions, during World War II, in willful altruistic suicides. Less well known are the accounts of other Japanese suicide clusters.

During the 1930s, hundreds of Japanese threw themselves into a volcanic crater on the small island of Mihara-Vama. This cluster occurred after a nineteen-year-old girl took a boat out to the island, climbed the mountain to the crater's edge, and jumped. In 1935, the government was able to stop the deaths by screening boat passengers to the island.

Rather than face the feared humiliation of capture, as well as the rumored murder, torture, and rape at the hands of the Americans, one thousand Japanese soldiers and civilians—adults and children—threw themselves from two cliffs on Saipan in the Northern Mariana Islands when U.S. troops took control of the island in 1944. As whole families jumped into the foaming seas, Americans in small boats offshore broadcast pleas for the Japanese not to commit suicide, and tried to save the few who had not yet drowned. Today, these sites, named Banzai and Suicide, are frequent stops for Japanese tourists who wish to honor the dead.

Early in November 1986, Japanese newspapers were dominated by coverage of a cluster of seven women's suicides. The story began on 1 November when a man out for a walk discovered seven charred bodies on a Wakayama beach. The women were identified as members of a tiny church called the Friends of Truth, and it was learned they had killed themselves to follow their religious leader who had died in a hospital the night before. They ranged in age from twenty-five to sixty-seven, and included the wife of the cult leader, and some of his blood relatives. The papers were fascinated with the deaths' parallels to the ancient Japanese feudal practice of *junshi*, in which retainers would follow their lords in death as an act of supreme loyalty.

Ebeye

Micronesia is located in the western Pacific. Four great archipelagos make up the area: the Carolinas, the Marianas, the Marshalls, and the Gilberts. Most people recognize the name of one island in the region, Guam, but the rest of the islands are known only to Americans and Europeans who served there in World War II, or have vacationed there since then. In the Marshalls, there exists a beautiful little island named Ebeye. Only one-eighth of square mile in size, some six thousand people are crowded onto it.

In 1967, Ebeye was hit by a suicide cluster. In November, the son of one of Ebeye's most important and wealthy families hanged himself. Apparently, this twenty-nine-year-old fellow was very intense, and maintained two families, each with a one-month-old daughter. He kept his dual life a secret from each family, and ran back and forth between his wives. The strain became too much for him, and he ended his life in what was to become known as a "lover's dilemma" suicide. Three days after this young man's suicide, a twenty-two-year-old male who was said to be "having problems with his wife," took his own life.

Since 1967, cluster suicides have haunted Ebeye. In the twenty years since the first case, many young boys have dreamed about the first man who killed himself, and have said that he was calling them to kill themselves. The anthropologist W.J. Alexander, who studied on Ebeye in the 1970s, recalled that "several suicide victims and several who have recently attempted suicide reported having a vision in which a boat containing all the past victims circles the island, with the deceased inviting the potential victims to join them. Many have." Indeed, they have: twenty-five completed suicides and scores of attempts from 1967 through 1980.

Donald H. Rubinstein, another anthropologist who examined the series, noted that the suicides came in clusters of three or four over the course of a few months, and then there would be no suicides for a year or more. They would occur within a small circle of friends. There were cases of suicides happening at the graveside of a friend. Suicide pacts among teenage friends also were reported. Rubinstein felt that the "meanings and significance of the suicides must therefore be understood at least partly in the context of these processes of modeling and contagion."

Frighteningly, Rubinstein and others observed that a "suicide subculture"—where, for example, boys especially would experiment with hanging themselves—was developing on some of the surrounding islands. Some boys said that they were as young as eight years old when they saw or heard about a suicide. Their curiosity about suicides has made the phenomenon an integrated part of the culture of Micronesia, and led to such articles as the one featured in the October 1986 issue of *National Geographic*, noting that the area has one of the highest suicide rates for young males in the world.

Jonestown

The most frequently discussed modern mass suicide is the one at Jonestown, Guyana. Jonestown was like a nine-hundred acre island cut out of the thick South American jungle. It was there that the Reverend James Warren Jones relocated his People's Temple from the San Francisco area. On 18 November 1978, supposedly frightened by the investigative visit of Congressman Leo Ryan, Jim Jones ordered Larry Schact, a medical school graduate and designated camp doctor, to prepare a cyanide-laced vat of strawberry Flavour-aide. Then, with guards at his side, Jones had his followers drink the "potion" and kill themselves. The death toll stood at 913 by most counts. Meanwhile, at the Guyanese airstrip near Jonestown, Jones had Ryan and his media contingent killed.

People could not believe the news accounts were true. The specter of Jonestown still fills the newspapers. During September 1986, one of Jones's assistants, Larry Layton, was standing trial for his involvement in the Jonestown incidents. The events of that November are thus being kept vividly alive by newspaper accounts of such court cases, and a made-for-television movie.

Mindanao

Six hundred miles southeast of Manila, the Philippines, is the island Mindanao. Hidden deep in its jungles is the village of Gunitan. The location can be reached only by hiking up rugged trails through thick forests. The village is at the base of the 9,540-foot Mount Apo, the highest mountain in the Philippines.

Living in Gunitan are the mountain people, the Ata, known in the Mindanao city of Davao as a "very peaceful" people who wore loincloths, ate roots, and hunted animals with bows and arrows. On 9 September 1985, the Ata's High Priestess Mangayanon Butaos, like Jim Jones of the People's Temple, convinced members of her mountain tribe to kill themselves. She promised them they would see God if they ate the poisoned food she offered them, and sixty-nine died soon after eating it. Survivors said they were forced to partake of porridge laced with insecticide. Reportedly, Butaos stabbed herself to death after the food was eaten by her followers.

Civilian offficals trying to reach the scene on 14 September turned back because of the stench of decaying flesh. Later, a team of militiamen who got into the area found dead bodies ripped apart by wild boars and bogs. When they finally reached the village of Gunitan, they counted sixty bodies, although the survivors of the mass suicide said sixty-nine people had decided to take their own lives because of Butaos's prophecies. Authorities speculated the other corpses probably were destroyed by animals.

The Fiery Clusters of the 1960s and 1970s

HISTORICALLY, suicide by fire—self-incineration—has often led to widespread copying and clustering. As mentioned earlier, groups of Russian *soshigateli* burned themselves to death in the last century. The modern era has seen many varieties of suicide clusters. Perhaps none have been as dramatic as those that have been extremely political, and therefore strikingly newsworthy conflagrations.

Historians and suicidologists generally classify the recent fiery clusters according to the country of origin, and the alleged political source of the protest. To Americans, the most important and memorable self-incinerations took place during the Vietnam Era.

The Burning Monks

During the early days of 1963, the ongoing Indochinese war was made more complex by the dictatorial policies of the Ngo Dinh Diem regime of South Vietnam. This American-backed government was led by the members of the Diem family, all Roman Catholics, who, the country's Buddhists felt, were extremely repressive. In Hue, South Vietnam, on 8 May, during a demonstration against the Diem policies, government troops fired on the crowd, killing nine Buddhists. In a country that was seventy percent Buddhist, the resulting protests were frequent and widespread. On 11 June 1963, the protests would take a new form, which would influence political suicides for two decades.

On that date, the Buddhist monk Thich Quang Duc doused his yellow robes with gasoline in the public square of Saigon and set himself on fire. Thousands watched, and Buddhist nuns and monks carried banners demanding religious freedom and social justice. The media had been forewarned that a demonstation was to take place, but they had not known that a monk would burn himself alive. The next day, photographs and films of the event were published and broadcast worldwide. Thich Quang Duc's dramatic declaration of dissent was headlined around the world.

During the summer of 1963, others in Vietnam chose to kill themselves in protest of the Diem regime. On 7 July, Vietnam's most famous writer, Nguyen Tuong Tam, a Buddhist, killed himself in prison by taking poison. Thich Quang Duc's act was viewed as the more dramatic, and soon imitated by others. On 4 August, a second Buddhist monk, in his twenties, Le, burned himself to death in the center of the seacoast town of Phan Thiet. Government troops removed his charred body before his fellow monks could reach it.

The self-incinerations spread quickly. On 13 August, a seventeen-year-old novice monk burned himself to death. Two days later, a Buddhist nun named Dieu Quang set herself on fire in the seacoast town of Ninh Hoa and died shortly thereafter. The next day, a seventy-one-year-old monk took his own life by burning in Hue's biggest pagoda. Three Buddhists had died by fire in one week. Government troops declared martial law in Hue, and were searching for ways to stop the suicides. But the political repression caused a renewed sense of outrage on the part of the Buddhists, and protests abounded.

By the end of the year, at least four other monks had burned themselves to death. In 1964 and 1965, nine political protest self-incinerations occurred; these included five Buddhist monks in South Vietnam, one politician in Korea, and three Americans.

The American self-incinerations began with Alice Herz, an eighty-two-year-old Quaker and librarian. She poured cleaning fluid over herself and set it afire on 17 March 1965, on a street corner in Detroit. Covered with second-degree and third-degree burns, as she was rushed to the hospital, she told a firefighter: "I did it to protest the arms race all over the world. I wanted to burn myself like the monks in Vietnam did." In her purse, police found a note stating Herz was protesting "the use of his high office by our President, L.B.J., in trying to wipe out small nations. . . . I wanted to call attention to this problem by choosing the illuminating death of a Buddhist."

Norman Morrison, thirty-two, also a Quaker, burned himself to death on 2 November 1965, in front of the Pentagon in Washington, D.C., because of the Vietnam conflict. Eight days later, twenty-two-year-old Catholic Worker Movement member Roger Allen LaPorte calmly went to the wide avenue in front of the United Nations, doused himself with gasoline from a gallon can, stepped off the curb, and sat cross-legged in the fashion of the Buddhist monks. He struck a match and was engulfed in flames. As he was rushed away, between asking for water repeatedly, LaPorte told the ambulance attendants: "I'm a Catholic Worker. I'm against war, all wars. I did this as a religious action." One of LaPorte's ambitions had always been to be a Trappist monk, and beginning in 1963, he had attended for a year the St. John Vianney Seminary in Barre, Vermont. As LaPorte lay dying on a hospital operating table, he was visited by two psychiatrists who asked him if he wanted to live. Unable to speak now because of a tube down his throat, he nodded affirmatively. He died the next day.

The highly visible protest suicides of Herz, Morrison, and LaPorte appear to have influenced the method of suicides for other Americans not so politically motivated during this same time period. For example, the day that LaPorte died, a South Bend, Indiana, woman attempted to commit suicide by fire. Despondent over the October death of her three-month-old baby, and the casualty reports from Vietnam, Celene Jankowski, twenty-four, set herself ablaze in front of her home. A police spokesperson noted that one of Jankowski's brothers had been killed in the Korean War, and she had been deeply disturbed by the Vietnam situation, although she was not a member of any formal protest organization.

The wave of political self-incinerations continued in 1966 and 1967. Thirteen Buddhists in Vietnam, one Soviet citizen, and one American student received widespread publicity during 1966 for their acts. In 1967, five Buddhists in Southeast Asia and five Americans in the U.S. died in fiery political protests. Three other Americans died by self-incineration between 1966 and 1967, but apparently not for political reasons. Still the contagion effect may be important in terms of these suicides.

Indeed, throughout the early 1970s, self-incinerations related to the Vietnam War continued in Southeast Asia and America. Times Square was the scene of a dramatic self-incineration when Hin Chi Yeung poured two cans of gasoline on himself and struck a match at 2 P.M. on Saturday, 18 July 1970. On 24 August 1971, a thirty-seven-year-old Vietnam veteran and father of six, Nguyen Minh Dang, set himself afire in Saigon's central market, praying for another veteran who burned himself to death on 16 August in a peace protest. A fifty-eight-year-old laborer at Vietnam's Tan Son Nhut Air Base burned himself to death "for the cause of national peace" on 6 September 1974.

The dramatic death of the Buddhist monk Thich Quang Duc forever changed the face of political protest. As researchers Kevin Crosby, Joonh-Oh Rhee, and J. Holland noted in analyzing suicides by fire for the years 1790 to 1972, seventy-one percent of the reported self-incinerations occurred in the last ten-year period. The rise and actual clustering of this form of suicide began only after the death of Thich Quang Duc in 1963. These researchers attempt "to explain the clusters of protest self-incinerations in South Vietnam" by pointing to the "high level of tension among the opposing factions" and the "intense emotional atmosphere" it produced. They felt similar clusters are likely to recur when times are "unsettled, emotions inflamed and when no appropriate outlet exists for the expression of commonly shared emotions." And we might add that the swift electronic distribution of the strikingly graphic pictures and written descriptions of the self-incinerations presented potential suicide victims with a collective method and model for behavior. Since 1963, the explosive nature of strained emtional times has produced other fiery clusters.

Czechoslovakia

In August 1968, the invasion of Czechoslovakia by the Soviet Union was met by a wave of international upset. But the outrage did not really come to a head until Jan Palach startled passersby by pouring a liquid over his body at about 3 P.M. on 16 January 1969, and then setting himself ablaze. The twenty-one-year-old student chose the statue of Wenceslas, the Czech hero saint, as the site of his protest in Prague. Palach had left a note declaring that he belonged to a group whose members planned to self-incinerate themselves, one every ten days, until the Soviet troops departed. Palach's protest and death three days later got worldwide media coverage, and others did follow his lead. At least seven people in Czechoslovakia, Scotland, and Hungary committed political suicide by fire after Palach's death. Reports of seven other self-incinerations, perhaps nonpolitical in nature, came from India, Pakistan, England, and the United States.

France and Thoughts of Biafra

Late in the 1960s, children were starving to death in the small African territory of Biafra. The pictures from the area were disturbing, and school children throughout the world showed much concern for these war and famine victims. But in France, suicide by fire was seen as the only form of protest that might end the suffering.

In January 1970, exactly one year to the day since Jan Palach had burned himself to death, a sixteen-year-old boy in the northern French city of Lille doused himself with gasoline and set himself ablaze in his high school playground. He had written on his notepaper: "I offer myself to atone for the wrongs committed in Biafra, against war, violence and the folly of men." Four days later, a nineteen-year-old boy burned himself to death in his nearby Lille schoolyard. He left a note which read: "I did it because I cannot adapt myself to this world. I did it as a sign of protest against violence, to see love again." In various parts of France, two days later, two men died by fiery suicides, and another made an attempt. Then, on 24 January, a seventeen-year-old girl set herself on fire at a Roman Catholic high school in a wealthy section of Paris, and jumped to her death from the fourth story.

Five self-incinerations took place in one week. In the two weeks after the first youth's death, six other youths died by fiery suicides. For the entire year of 1970, sixteen cases of suicide by fire are known to have occurred in France with ten of them clustering during the month of January.

The English and Welsh Epidemic

Between October 1978 and October 1979, eighty-two people, mostly young single men, and older married women, died by burning themselves to death in England and Wales. These suicides by fire were not seen by researchers John Ashton and Stuart Donnan as primarily political protests, but merely as an epidemic stimulated by one such fiery death.

Late in September 1978, Lynette Phillips, a twenty-four-year-old Australian heiress, was arrested in London and deported after she said she was going to kill herself in Parliament Square. Phillips was a member of PROUT, the Progressive Utilization Theory, an Asian-based religious sect. PROUT had developed out of a political and religious conflict with the Gandhi leadership of India, and had been involved in protests against that government's outlawing of PROUT in India, and at Indian consulates in Australia and England. By the time Phillips was deported, seven PROUT members had burned themselves to death.

On 2 October 1978, Phillips set herself afire in front of the Palais de Nations in Geneva, Switzerland. Her statement made it clear she had committed suicide to change more speedily the world order.

Three days after the Phillips suicide, Pamela Evans Cooper followed suit on the banks of the Thames at Windsor. By the end of the month, England and Wales were in the midst of a full-scale self-incineration cluster. Ten people had died by burning. Reports in the English media noted six similar suicides throughout the Commonwealth: three in New Zealand, two in Australia, and one in India.

Soon after the start of this cluster, suicide researchers Ashton and Donnon noted the potential beginnings of an epidemic and began obtaining death certificates and coroners' reports. They then discovered the extent of the self-burnings. Later, after analyzing all the data, they wrote: "What we have called an epidemic is, we think, an example of the phenomenon of imitation. . . . There can be little doubt that the spread of this specific epidemic must have been mediated by news coverage; deaths occurring in this manner tend to be widely reported."

The English and Welsh suicides by fire decreased as 1979 came to an end. The notion of political protest by self-incineration does not appear to be as important during the 1980s as it was in the 1960s and 1970s. With a few minor exceptions, as in Korea for example, during May 1986, suicide clusters by fire seem to be on the decline.

Clusters of a Stressful Age

OCCURRING within a short period of time, usually within the same community, suicide clusters would not seem easy to ignore. However, most suicides appear as random individual acts, and are thus not readily linked to each other. One reason that some mysterious waves of suicides are noticed is because certain collections of deaths are all of one specific age group, such as with the teen suicide clusters. But several series have been clustered around other characteristics, such as death by a particular method, as in the previous chapter. Another common accumulator of suicides is the similar stressful lifestyle of the victims, be they town fathers, policemen, gays, or farmers.

The Town Fathers' Suicides

Frequently, modern clusters of suicides appear among individuals in similar walks of life, having comparable demographics, including age. Such people having the same lifestyles often carry analogous burdens in similar ways, and sometimes decide suicide is the only way out.

Take, for example, what happened in a little town some eighteen miles west of Cologne in 1973 and 1974. Residents of the village of Dueren were shocked and baffled by a series of suicides among the town's well-known figures. The cluster began on 19 October, when one of Dueren's leading doctors shot himself in the head. Ten weeks later, a notary hanged himself in his offce. Then late in January, the chief physician at the local hospital took poison and was found dead. On 5 February, the fourth suicide took place when a prominent local official chose death by hanging. Local police said all four men knew each other, and had in common their reportedly happy home lives and comfortable incomes.

The reasons behind these suicides are uncertain, but the fact that all of these town fathers used suicide as their last option sadly reflects the reality that people in stressful situations frequently feel like pawns of fate. Policemen are a current case in point.

Police Clusters

Occupations naturally pigeonhole people, so when a grouping of suicides begins to appear among fellow employees, notice is taken. During 1986, in two large American cities on the East Coast, people started talking about the wave of suicides among the police. During one tragic week in April, three Boston policemen shot themselves to death. The chain of events began on 11 April, when twenty-nine-year veteran patrolman Edward Foley, fifty-six, killed himself. He was found in his home. Sadly, one friend noted, Foley was scheduled to retire in six months. A Police Department spokesperson called it, "an accidental shooting." On 17 April, when two officers assigned to the same Area D headquarters killed themselves, no one was talking about anything but suicide.

Clovis Cobb, thirty-four, a seventeen-year veteran of the force, was pronounced dead after he was found with a gunshot wound to the left chest in his car on Dorchester Avenue near Field's Corner. Cobb, a patrolman, was killed by his own gun, a nonservice revolver, which he carried in a shoulder holster. An hour later, another policeman killed himself. Saul Shamjowicz, thirty-three, with eight years on the force, was discovered in his Randolph, Massachusetts, home, dead from a gunshot wound. Shamjowicz, a detective, used his service revolver.

The three Boston deaths were followed the next month by yet

another police-related suicide. On 23 May 1986, William C. Parsons, sixty-two, a former Metropolitan District Commission police officer working at Boston's Suffolk Downs as a private detective, killed himself. Parsons collapsed in a stadium restroom after a gunshot rang out at about 2 P.M. He had shot himself in the head. Eddie Donovan, the director of the Boston Police Department's stress program, said he had never seen a cluster of possible suicides so close together in his twenty-nine years at the department.

During September 1986, police suicides were the talk of New York City. On 9 September, after being arrested for drunken driving at the scene of an accident in which his passenger was killed, Officer Michael J. McNamara, twenty-eight, snatched a gun from a county officer and killed himself. He was a five-year veteran of a police mounted unit. A few hours later, Officer Thomas Lucas, thirty years old, reported to work, calmly walked into a bathroom stall of his Flushing, Queens, police precinct, and fatally shot himself in the temple. No one knew why.

Between January and mid-September 1986, New York City had experienced seven police suicides. That was up considerably from the five in 1985, and three each in 1983 and 1984. Concern was generated by the suicides, and self-examinations by the police occurred throughout the fall. As one officer, Steven Rubino of the Thirty-second Precinct in Harlem said: "The guy on the street, we can handle that. The pressures come from within. . . . We're constantly reminded that we're on duty twenty-four hours a day. You fear the person on the street, you fear your boss, you fear for your children because you know the violence of the world. The pressures just never end."

For yet another New York policeman, the pressures were too much for him early in 1987. On 14 January, Detective Lieutenant John Gaggin, a top official in the Suffolk County Police Department, shot himself to death only hours before he was to testify before the State Investigation Commission. Lieutenant Gaggin's squad was under examination regarding allegations of brutality in a 1985 case of mistaken arrest. Described as an "intense guy" and a "stickler for detail" by his commanding officer, Commissioner DeWitt C. Treder, Gaggin apparently felt the pressures of the job more acutely than his fellows.

"If someone is watching you all the time when you are trying to do your job, it's very difficult to continue," Treder observed. "We've had this monkey on our backs for more than a year. The men just want to put it behind us and get [the investigators] off our backs."

Police in Canada have committed suicide because of similar stresses. In September 1986, Royal Canadian Mounted Police officers released the letter of a fellow officer who had killed himself. He was a man thirty-eight years old, and had been on the force half his life. "I am getting burned out," he wrote, acknowledging he needed to get help to cope with the stress of a job that he loved, even though it caused him to neglect his wife and kids.

In general, the assumption has been that police are under a great deal more stress than the rest of the population, and thus have a higher rate of suicide. The classical study of police suicides conducted by Friedman looked at New York City police suicides from 1934 to 1940. What he found was an incredibly high rate, an average of eighty per one hundred thousand. Other early studies also showed high rates. But other research does not demonstrate such extremely elevated numbers. For example, Dr. Robert Loo's new 1986 study of the Royal Canadian Mounted Police showed a rate "much lower than both the comparable Canadian rate and the high rates reported for some American police forces."

What researchers on police suicides have apparently overlooked is the wide ranging influence of behavior contagion among the close comrades of the force, yet no one is currently studying this factor. That police suicides actually do cluster seems to be quite apparent from an anecdotic overview of the problem, and further study and statistical examinations should be undertaken. For now, we know suicide clusters do occur among the men and women in blue, but we do not know how frequently.

Gays, AIDS, and Suicide

During the 1980s, professionals around the U.S. began hearing reports of a hidden suicide cluster of gay men suffering from acquired immune deficiency syndrome, AIDS. Because of the secretive nature of homosexuality in America, only casual accounts of this special kind of gay suicide are available to date.

University of California at San Francisco researchers Peter Goldblum and Jeffrey Moulton have written that the scope of AIDS-related suicides is "unknown due to the lack of epidemiological data. However, the numerous anecdotal reports from across the United

States and . . . San Francisco . . . indicate that suicide is, indeed, a salient issue in AIDS." They further write in the November 1986 issue of the AIDS Health Project publication, *FOCUS*, that the San Francisco medical examiner believes that from six to twelve people with AIDS committed suicide there in 1985. Furthermore, the Hospice of San Francisco has documented from October 1984 to April 1986 thirteen attempts and six completed AIDS-related suicides. That city's Shanti Project identified eighteen people at serious suicidal risk, and one completed suicide during a six-week period, February to March 1986. The San Francisco Suicide Prevention Center currently says it gets sixty to one hundred AIDS-related calls per month.

In 1972, when the article "Dual Suicide in Homosexuals" was published in the *Journal of Nervous and Mental Disorders*, the phenomenon of gays killing themselves together was noted. The doctors who wrote that study felt that "it was conceivable that dual suicides among homosexuals may be more common than has been reported. In fact, the authors have been informed of other cases appearing in the emergency rooms of big city hospitals that have not been reported."

Therefore, when suicidologists started hearing about the AIDS-related suicides, little surprise was registered that, indeed, an epidemic of suicides was occurring. Like the plague victims during the Middle Ages, some AIDS patients decided suicide was a solution to their bleak future. One of the most graphic examples of this occurred on 24 October 1985. On that day, Charles Villalonga, forty-three, an AIDS victim, and his companion, Gilbert Rodriguez, forty-four, tied themselves at the waist with a silk sash, and jumped out of their thirty-fifth-floor apartment window to their deaths. They had filled their New York City apartment with flowers, and toasted each other with an expensive wine before their suicides.

With the commencement of the military's testing of its personnel, the phenomenon spread to the services. A case in point happened at the Walter Reed Medical Center early in 1986. An army private undergoing medical tests for AIDS at the hospital hanged himself with his bootlaces in a stairwell. Reports indicate the patient had been subjected to taunts and harassment by non-AIDS patients.

The clustering of AIDS victims' suicides, because of the controversial social, emotional, and political nature of AIDS and its mostly gay victims, has until recently, remained relatively unexamined. However, the time has come for a major study to obtain an overview and understanding of the wave of suicides of people who have the modern plague, AIDS. Until then, we must at least observe that something suicidal is happening among yet another distinctive population group.

Farmer Suicides

The morning dawned as it usually did at the Burr farm on 9 December 1985. The two-story, shuttered, white home of Dale and Emily Burr stood about eight miles from Hills, Iowa, in the middle of some of the most beautiful farmland in America. But hard times had fallen on agriculture in the U.S., and murder-suicide was soon to visit the Burrs.

On that Monday morning in December, Emily Burr had just finished washing the breakfast dishes, and had put out a package of frozen ground beef for a later meal. She had started frosting some of the cookies she had just baked when Dale appeared at the top of the basement stairs, a .12 gauge pump shotgun in hand. He shot her once in the chest. Friends and neighbors later would say the couple never fought and loved each other deeply. People found insights into his motives in the note he left and his later actions. The penciled message on the back of an old envelope was addressed to Burr's only son, John: "I'm sorry, I can't take the problems anymore."

Burr jumped into his green-and-white Chevy pickup truck and drove to the Hills Bank & Trust Company, the holder of Burr's mortgage, chatted in an easygoing fashion with some folks inside, told people to have a nice day, left, but soon returned with his shotgun concealed. Burr then killed the bank president, John Hughes, forty-six, who years earlier had been Burr's first loan officer. Burr had been worried about the bank foreclosing on his farm, and several days earlier had told some relatives he was being pressured by the bank to sell livestock and machinery. Burr's fear of losing the farm, and inability to manage his debt, many folks later would say, is what drove him to these acts of murder.

Next Burr went to the farm of Richard Goody. Goody, thirty-eight, had recently won a $6,626.96 court settlement against John Burr over rights to some leased land. For a decade before the land dispute, the Burrs and Goody had been neighbors and friends. Burr talked to Goody that cold winter day and before the words got heated, Goody turned away. Burr pulled the shotgun out of the cab of his truck, and shot Goody dead with a blast to the face. At that moment, Marilyn Goody and her six-year-old son pulled into the Goody driveway, saw what had happened, then frantically got their pickup out of the farmyard. From inside Marilyn Goody's truck cab, she could hear buckshot hitting her vehicle's tailgate. She raced to the police and told them what had happened.

Three Johnson County deputies had been sent out to find Burr, but Officer David Henderson was the first to see him. Henderson followed Burr for two miles before he turned on his siren and lights. At that point, Burr pulled onto an icy back road, and parked on its shoulder. Henderson called for a backup officer and waited until he arrived. Carefully going to the truck's cab, they found Burr slumped over, dead. The butt of the shotgun was braced against the passenger's floorboard, the barrel aimed at his chest. A later autopsy would show that Burr had to shoot himself twice, as the first shot ended up under his left arm. In deep pain, Burr must have had to use his right hand to eject the spent shell, and place a new cartridge in the chamber. Then he must have repositioned the gun and pulled the trigger again. The blast hit him in the heart.

The people of the area had liked Dale Burr a great deal. He was a sincere fellow with a robust laugh and a good nature. Folks could put the pieces together only by looking at the farm crisis around them.

Dale Burr's rampage startled the nation. "Indebted farmer kills 3, then self," shouted the headlines. The farm crisis had turned bloody. Although rising farmer debt and low commodity prices were a regular feature of the evening news, Dale Burr was a flesh-and-blood example of the human stress of the farm crisis. He was more than a half million dollars in debt, and was going to be driven off the farm his family had owned since 1879. Dale Burr made the "tragedy waiting to happen," so often mentioned by debt-ridden farmers, actually occur.

Farmer suicide clusters have become part of the America of the 1980s. In the days following the news of the Burr murder-suicide, the upper Midwest experienced a concentrated wave of similar cases. For example, on 8 January 1986, Union County, South Dakota, Farmers Home Administration Supervisor Bruce Litchfield, thirty-eight, shot three members of his Elk Point family and then committed suicide. Within twenty-four hours, Alcester Police Chief Tony Lee shot his wife before turning the gun on himself. Union County

Sheriff Bud Rasmussen was puzzled by the deaths, especially after two teens killed themselves in February.

Since Dale Burr killed his wife, his banker, his neighbor, and himself, suicidologists have turned their attention to the epidemic of farmer suicides. At the University of Minnesota, public health officials announced in March 1986 that a six-state (Minnesota, Iowa, Montana, North Dakota, South Dakota, and Wisconsin) study of farmer suicides would be undertaken. Paul Gunderson, chief of statistics at the Minnesota Department of Health noted that between thirty and fifty of the four hundred Minnesota suicides each year are from farm families.

Meanwhile, in Manitoba, a similar study did show a connection between the poor farm economy and the increased suicide rate. Dr. Jim Walker, head of the psychology department at Brandon University, talked of Manitoba farmers: "I would say that this is a group that is dealing with a very high level of stress. It goes hand in hand with the economy. I see a lot of people pretty depressed about the whole farm situation. There's a link between depression and suicide. Farmers are strong, resilient, reserved, quiet types of people. They keep things bottled up and suffer in silence. That's part of the problem."

The Spurious, Curious, and Dubious

IN RESEARCHING the literature and history of suicide clusters, a great deal of strange material has been uncovered. Indeed, some of these branching side trails are very bizarre. Some are curious items that may have some factual basis. Still others are doubtful reports of a mildly intriguing nature.

The purpose of this chapter is to explore and expose a few of the more prominent tales, to put them to rest, and thus to lessen the impact of these detractors from the serious study of suicide clusters. We feel these records need to be chronicled to warn the cautious reader or the inquiring researcher of the pitfalls in the research of this matter. In the process, this chapter will diverge from the more traditional and tragic narratives that populate the accounts of suicide clusters, epidemics, and mass deaths, and venture a quick look at some of these spurious, curious, and dubious accounts of supposed suicide groupings.

Animal Suicide Clusters

Most authors in suicidology quite clearly state that they feel animals do not possess a consciousness on the level of human beings, and thus cannot commit suicide. This, however, has not stopped the public and popular writers from discussing the notion of animal suicides.

The belief that animals may kill themselves is especially prevalent with regard to the mass deaths of dolphins and whales. The elementary understanding of the problem is portrayed by the title of a recent *Omni* article, "Whale Suicides."

Mass beachings of small whales have occurred routinely, at least since the time of the Greeks. Aristotle was mystified by the deaths. Modern scientists are as well. The Smithsonian has a hotline to deal with the strandings, and biologists travel hundreds of miles to study the phenomenon. They come away from their investigations without clear-cut answers. Some believe the beachings are caused by parasites in the inner ear of the whales which disorient them. Others feel that dolphins hit a thermal wall, an imaginary dividing line between two masses of cold and warm water. Still other researchers think magnetic or early primordial reasoning is behind the beachings. In the fall of 1986, strandings and deaths of dozens of dolphins off Cape Cod were blamed on a flu virus. But no one is sure of the answer.

Most contemporary thoughts about suicide as an explanation for the death of the small cetaceans appear to date from the late 1960s and early 1970s when Dr. John Lilly was working with dolphins. A well-written article by Cleveland Amory, published in 1970, dealt with Lilly's work, and was headlined, "After Living with Man, a Dolphin May Commit Suicide." Amory quoted Lilly as simply noting that after his Virgin Islands dolphin work had been going on for some time, the animals began "committing suicide." After the dolphins had developed a close personal relationship with various members of Lilly's staff, they seemed unable to cope without these people. Because of personnel departures and his growing uneasiness with the navy-sponsored experiments he had to conduct, Lilly terminated the project. Shortly thereafter, he brought a dolphin named Peter back to a Miami aquarium, and, according to Lilly: "Two weeks later he committed suicide. . . . In a period of two months, five of them committed suicide. Apparently they knew the project was coming to an end." They committed suicide by going to the bottom of their enclosed tanks, and drowning themselves.

Since the time of Lilly's work and Amory's article, each stranding of whales or beaching of dolphins is greeted with some hint from the media that the event was a suicide cluster. For now, until we know more about the intelligence and consciousness of cetaceans, their motivations will have to remain a mystery.

Another kind of mass death of animals has also been treated as suicidal in nature. That of the deaths of mammals by jumping over cliffs into the valleys or seas below. For example, on Friday, 24 July 1970, Reuters news service reported "1050 Alpine Sheep Commit Mass Suicide" at Tignes, France, by leaping to their death from a five-hundred-foot cliff. Shepherds in Reggio Emilia, northern Italy, were baffled in December 1978, when two hundred sheep drowned after jumping into a swift river. In December 1985, Israeli scientists were perplexed because hundreds of mice were "committing suicide" by jumping off cliffs in the Golan Heights. One hundred and fifty were counted at the bottom of one precipice.

These published press stories appear to be merely a more recent version of the sad and sorrowful story of the lemmings who periodically, as one leading magazine once put it, go "pattering to their doom" from the mountains of Norway by throwing themselves en masse into the swirling ocean. But as naturalist Ivan T. Sanderson has written: "This makes a nice story, pointing a poignant moral, but unfortunately it is almost complete rubbish."

As Sanderson and others have noted, the tales of lemmings, mice, and other animals jumping from cliffs in "mass suicides" are more related to the effect of food supply and demand, and fertility rates, than to any suicidal urges. As the population booms, the food supply becomes low, and the animals start migrating outward in all directions. In the case of the lemmings in Norway, some eventually come down the mountains, and residents near the fjords observe the seemingly strange behavior of hundreds of little volelike creatures, jumping into the ocean and rivers, trying to swim to the other side in search of food. Literally, hundreds of them drown. The folklore of the death march of the lemmings has developed out of this chain of events. Like the panic of sheep, the food search of rodents has nothing to do with suicide.

Custer's Last Stand

On 25 June 1876, according to the traditional view of the events, a large combined force of Sioux and Cheyenne, led by Sitting Bull, annihilated Lieutenant Colonel George Armstrong Custer and his

Seventh Cavalry at Little Bighorn, Montana. Outnumbered ten to one, some 266 soldiers are said to have been slaughtered.

In the June 1986 issue of *Natural History*, authors Douglas D. Scott and Melissa A. Connor detail their archaeological research on the site of the Battle of Little Bighorn. One passage is especially intriguing. In their analysis of an almost complete find from one individual they mention that as this soldier "was dead or dying, someone also shot him in the head with a Colt revolver." The researchers then go on to state that "the archaeological data support much in the Indian accounts of the battle and contradict none of them." Here they mean to say that the textbook history has been supported largely through their research. But is the book closed?

Forensic scientist Jerry D. Spencer has noted that the Native American accounts, if heeded, may indicate something other than the usual notion of mass homicide: "One of the more interesting theories proposed to account for the death of Custer and his men was that they committed suicide en masse after they were surrounded by the Indians. This theory was advanced by Thomas B. Marquis, a physician assigned to the Cheyenne Indian Reservation during the late teens and early 1920s. In the process of ministering to the health needs of the Indians, Dr. Marquis interviewed a number of the survivors of the Custer battle and, from these Indian accounts, developed his theory."

Spencer wrote in the *Journal of Forensic Science* that Dr. Marquis was told that the Cheyenne and Sioux actually saw a group of twenty soldiers who had broken from Custer's ranks begin shooting themselves. "This action was in full view of the approximately two hundred troopers remaining on the hill. A short while later, the Indians heard considerable shooting on the hill, then nothing. Cautiously going up the hill, they found six or seven troopers still alive. They were quickly killed, and that was the end of the battle."

Marquis's mass suicide theory has not found favor with many experts in Western history, and his book on the subject was rejected by several publishers. It finally was published some forty years after his death. *Keep the Last Bullet for Yourself* has recently been revised and published again in 1985. Still, historians have trouble with his suicide theory. William Gillette, who teaches a course entitled "Cowboys and Indians" at Rutgers, in which he debunks many Wild West myths, recently wrote: "Regarding Custer, my first impression based on something I have read or heard is that the theory of mass suicide is farfetched but I can't give you a single reason why."

Although the article by Scott and Connor supports the general historical notion that Custer and his men were killed by the Cheyenne and Sioux, perhaps some open-minded examination of the evidence may someday confirm the reports of the Native Americans, as told to Dr. Marquis. Perhaps not. Scott later noted that he and Connor had examined only a small part of the archaeological data.

That Custer or his men were killed by their own hand is today a very bizarre theory, which must remain, for now, only a curious footnote in suicidology.

Comet Clusters

In 1909 to 1910 and 1985 to 1986, Halley's Comet visited this end of the solar system. For those interested in suicides, there are uncomfortable coincidences between the times of the visit of the comet and the rates of self-destruction during the two periods.

The year 1910 was marked by a teen suicide epidemic on a scale similar to the current one. Speaking in Portland, Maine, in 1985, the American Association of Suicidology's Chief Certifier, Dr. James Wells, observed: "The fact that adolescent suicide has risen 237 percent between 1960 and 1980 cannot be accounted for simply by better reporting techniques. The suicide rate now of about 12.1 per one hundred thousand is a little bit higher than it was back in 1910 when there was a lot of concern about adolescent suicide."

During June 1985, at the first National Conference on Youth Suicide in Washington, D.C., various speakers noted that seventy-five years earlier none other than Sigmund Freud had opened a similar conference in Vienna. As it turns out, Freud gave the introductory remarks for that Austrian conference, "On Suicide, Particularly Among Children," as well as the concluding ones. The meetings took place on 20 and 27 April 1910. Freud alluded to another speaker who had noted the "youthful suicides" were occurring "not only among pupils in secondary schools but also among apprentices and others." Facing a challenge close to that of many suicide prevention workers and researchers today, at the end of the conference, Freud soberly observed: "In spite of all the valuable material that has been brought before us in this discussion, we have not reached a decision on the problem that interests us."

Does Halley's Comet have anything to do with the "youthful suicides" of Freud's time? As Dr. Jerred Metz noted in his 1985 book on Halley's Comet, there is an astrosociology to be taken into account regarding the comet. Besides Mars and the rings of Saturn, most folks limit their passion for otherworldly objects to one specific item, Halley's Comet. This may be hard to believe, after its most disappointing recent visit, but many grew up holding it in awe.

Spurious connections between an astronomical event and human phenomenon must be guarded against, but with reference to some suicides and Halley's Comet, there was clear evidence of a connection in 1910. Back then, people the world over were scared to death of the impending close encounter with the comet. In their book, *The New York Times Guide to the Return of Halley's Comet*, the *Times* science writers entitled their chapter on the comet's last return: "1910: Will the Earth Survive?" Metz wrote, in his book: "May 18, 1910, was a day of dread." On that date, the Earth was to have passed through the supposed poisonous tail of the comet. The only solution to the anxiety of many was suicide. Records of suicide clusters in Japan, Italy, and Spain also show this. We are struck by Nigel Calder's insights on the matter. Calder, writing in *The Comet is Coming!*, noted: "Comets kill people by self-fulfilling superstition, when those who read them as telegrams from the gods or the Devil turn in panic to homicide or suicide."

In the United States, the chronicled attempts and completed suicides tend to be those clustering around 18 May 1910. Fearing no escape from the comet, Blanche Covington of Chicago locked herself in her room and turned on the gas. Her death is one of the most widely mentioned suicides said to be caused by Halley's Comet.

But there were other, less well-known American comet suicides. Sophie Houge, also of Chicago, killed herself by the same method as Blanche Covington, through the use of illuminating gas. Viola Gastenum of Anaheim, California, gave lye to her two children and swallowed some herself. This murder-suicide failed, and they all survived. Denver's Jeanette Niebert swallowed morphine on 18 May. According to the *Rocky Mountain News*, her last words were: "I think—the comet." Bessie Bradley, twenty-five, became so disturbed by all the various predictions that when the comet did not appear on 19 May, she turned on the gas and killed herself. On 21 May, W. J. Lord of Cottonwood, Alabama, was recovering from four attempts he had made on his own life. First he shot himself, then jumped off a roof, shortly thereafter tried to cut his own throat, and finally jumped in a well.

"Suicidal mania," as Dr. Metz labels it, was so widespread in

1910 that newspapers like the *Seattle Post-Intelligencer* carried the headline: "Fear of Annihilation Leads Weak-Minded to Suicide and Crime." The *New York Times* for 19 May 1910, ran this one: "Some Driven to Suicide, Others Become Temporarily Insane from Brooding over Comet."

There is no doubt about it: for some individuals in 1910, Halley's Comet caused fear and panic. And some people committed suicide based directly on their anxiety about the comet's effects. The strange synchronicity between comets and suicides perhaps belongs in the world of folklore and cycles, but hints of this special linkage are buried deep in the literature of comets.

Even Edmund Halley, the discoverer of the comet that carries his name, was touched by this weird synchronicity. On 5 March 1684, his father, Edmund Halley, Sr., walked out of the family house, and never returned. His body was found in a river at Temple Farm, near Rochester, Great Britain. In 1932, examining the evidence carefully, the distinguished Halley scholar Eugene Fairfield MacPike declared the death of the elder Halley a suicide.

Information on the lore of comets and suicide is easy to discover. The very word "disaster" evolved from "evil star," the ancients' way of talking about comets. The connection between disasters, specifically suicides, and comets goes way back. One such record is to be found in the Ipuwer Papyrus, "Admonitions of a Sage." According to that chronicle, in 1369 B.C., Egypt was visited by a huge comet and catastrophic events simultaneously. As the astronomers Victor Clube and Bill Napier noted when writing about this comet's appearance, many people were driven to suicide. And this tendency has continued down through history.

At the time of Jerusalem's war with Rome and many suicide clusters in A.D. 66, Halley's Comet hung like "a sword" over the city. Between 1347 and 1348, two comets blazed over Europe. During their visit, the Black Death appeared, and eventually killed twenty-five million people, a third of Europe's population. Mass suicides occurred throughout Europe. Earthquakes took place in Cyprus, Greece, and Italy. Doom and gloom was seen as related to these dual comets. Mass suicides and comets have also been associated in the years 1506, 1528 to 1529, 1582, and 1666.

In 1927, Comet Skjellerup appeared, and then Germany's "Black Friday" occurred; the economy collapsed and it was the beginning of a worldwide depression. Many related suicides occurred. Other disasters included the death of Ferdinand I, King of Romania; an earthquake in central Japan, leaving thousands dead; and floods in India, Siberia, Romania, New England, and Algeria, killing hundreds. All these disasters, in the public's mind, were somehow related to the appearance of the comet.

Shakespeare noted: "When beggars die, there are no comets seen; The heavens themselves blaze forth the death of princes."

Martin Luther commented: "The Heathen say that comets arise from natural causes, but God creates not a single comet that does not foreshadow a certain calamity."

Perhaps there is something to the links between comets and suicides, but more probably the comets often frame events they do not cause. Other spectacular comet appearances, however, seem to have influenced and affected some people. These people have committed suicide.

During the 1986 visit of Halley's Comet, the mythmaking regarding comet clusters continued. At an April presentation at the American Association of Suicidology Conference in Atlanta, I presented many of the ideas stated above in a lecture entitled "Comets and Suicides." Despite the straightforward tone of my talk, the news media decided to report my speech to fit the folklore of suicides and comets. Indeed, the *Las Vegas Sun*, in a front-page story, using two-inch headlines, proclaimed "Teen Suicide? Blame Halley." The phenomenon of teen suicides between 1985 and 1986 had nothing to do with the appearance of Halley's Comet, but it made a good story.

Part 2

"If youth is the season of hope, it is often so only in the sense that our elders are hopeful about us; for no age is so apt as youth to think its emotions, partings and resolves are the last of their kind."

—George Eliot, 1871

Today's Epidemic of Youth Suicide Clusters

THE PHENOMENON of youth suicide clusters is nothing new, as we have seen from the ancient records of the young women who hanged themselves in Miletus. However, only in recent years has the extent of the teen clusters been brought to the attention of a concerned populace. Systematically, and dramatically, it appears our young people are killing themselves in groups of threes and fives throughout the country.

The clusters of teen suicides appear to be on the increase, and only the lastest manifestation of the pressures of our times. As Susan and Daniel Cohen point out in their book, *Teenage Stress*, the tensions for today's adolescents come from a variety of sources: competition in school, fights at home, changes in physical appearance, drugs, sex, and dating. One result is suicide clusters.

In the next several pages, you will read the detailed accounts of some of this decade's most concentrated teen suicide clusters. Many of these clusters will be known to you, but by reading the full stories of the incidents, your picture of the events will be fuller than the brief newspaper accounts you might have run across. The names of the places where these clusters occurred may even be familiar: Plano, Clear Lake, Peekskill, Wind River, Spencer, Leominster, and Omaha. Some of them, like Mankato, may be less well known. These are the places, but what of the adolescents? What of the troubled lives of some of the teens who lived there? And what of the hidden patterns in these stories? Before we proceed, let us examine one: the timing of these clusters.

Among the general population, according to most records kept since the beginning of this century, the peak of suicides has occurred in May. Starting in the late spring, through the summer, autumn, and early winter, the number of suicides decreased until they reached a low point in December. Then the climb began anew in January, until reaching the high point in May.

Looking at the combined U.S. suicide statistics during the years 1972 to 1976, researcher Kenneth Bollen found that among all demographic groups, May still is the peak month, and December the low one. But his study showed that among the very specific age group, fifteen- to twenty-nine-year-olds, November was the peak and January the trough.

Examining closely the teen suicide clusters of 1983, 1984, 1985, and 1986, we discover something unique. Neither May nor November is the peak month for the special kind of adolescent suicides that occur in the midst of these clusters. Instead, February consistently turns up as the month of recurring importance. During February 1983, two teens in the space of seven days killed themselves in Plano, Texas, at the beginning of that cluster. Throughout the month of February 1984, southeastern New York experienced five teen suicides that signaled the start of that area's cluster, and Plano, Texas, registered another suicide, which may have demonstrated a repeating anniversary syndrome. In February 1985 a teen suicide television movie aired, and more teen suicides occurred in New York and Colorado. Finally, during February 1986, clusters of adolescent suicides and attempts broke out in Nebraska, Massachusetts, Minnesota, and South Dakota. And on 23 February 1986, in Plano, Texas, an eighteen-year-old committed suicide, exactly three years to the day after the town's first cluster suicide.

Why is February the month of suicide clusters? Is it because it follows the depressing and stressful time for some teens of family holidays, and unfulfilled vacation hopes? On 14 February 1984, in Putnam Valley, New York, Justin Spoonhour, fourteen, hanged himself. Because he committed suicide on Valentine's Day, his mother believed the date held a key to his death, as it highlighted for her son his loneliness. Has February's time of isolation been disturbing to these teens on a level we have overlooked? Whatever the reason, February is a high-risk time for clusters, and suicide prevention workers should be prepared for the worst from January through March. A smaller peak of clusters also appears to occur in August and September, perhaps having to do with the pressure of the start of school.

Teen suicide clusters have many lessons to teach us. Let us, therefore, turn to the in-depth examination of them.

Boomtown Pressures and the Texas Clusters

Plano, Texas

TWENTY MILES north of Dallas, twenty years ago, Plano was a small farming village of about three thousand folks. But in the last two decades the soybean and cotton fields have given way to the spread of housing subdivisions and shopping plazas. In 1970, the population numbered seventeen thousand. In 1980, it had reached seventy-two thousand; by 1983, almost ninety thousand, and by 1985, over one hundred twenty thousand. From all reports, the population has continued growing by ten thousand people a year.

Late in the 1970s, the *Los Angeles Times* said Plano was "the quintessential Sunbelt city," and *Texas Monthly* commented: "There stands on the Texas plains a perfect city." *Newsweek* in 1983 observed: "Plano is one of the 'pop-up' communities that began to dot the Sunbelt in the '70s, as upwardly mobile young executives in search of the good life moved in from the foundering cities of the East."

The city was far from perfect. The fast-paced, white collar suburb of Plano soon showed the darker side of high achievement. The number of divorces, previously low, jumped to one thousand a year in the early 1980s. Most people who had to come to Plano left because of the mobility inherent in their middle management jobs. Large segments of the populace had lived less than three years in the sprawling community when their teens began dying. After the deaths started, everyone started noticing the Sunbelt rootlessness, the competitive pressures, the incidence of substance abuse and alcoholism. But by then, it was too late for the children. Plano found itself in the grip of a suicide cluster.

It began with Bill Ramsey and Bruce Calvin. Their story is the story of Plano. Bruce and his family moved from Rochester, Michigan, in June 1982—their fifth move. That first summer, Bruce played with his computer and watched television sitcoms, usually "The Brady Bunch." In September, after he started Plano Senior High School, he met Bill Ramsey. They became fast friends, and hung out at places like the McDonald's near school and the popular local video arcade, Texas Time Out, TTO. They became known as "the Two Bs." They were fun to be around and seemed to enjoy themselves a lot.

But then something happened to Bill, reportedly, after he saw the movie, *Pink Floyd—the Wall*. The movie is about a rock star's construction of a wall around himself. Bill began to build his own wall. Soon Bill took to wearing boots and a leather jacket. He also started writing dark poems he would share with Bruce, such as:

Death is painless, quick
As a whisper on the wind
Silently calling.

Bruce got a leather jacket also.

On 19 February 1983, Bill, Bruce, and another friend, Chris Thornsberry, met at a local pizza joint, Chuck E. Cheese's. Like TTOs, it was filled with video games, and the noise of rock music. The Two Bs and Chris decided to have a drag race. It was Chris's 1973 Corvette against Bruce's 1972 Skylark, out on one of the long and hot blacktops that line the country around Plano. Bill, with flag in hand, was set to give the signal letting them know when to let it rip.

But then something bizarre happened. Bruce's car never left the starting line, and Chris's Corvette swerved and struck Bill. Chri[illegible] started screaming, "Bill, are you all right? Are you all right? Bill, [illegible] you all right?" Bill Ramsey, seventeen, was not all right. Rushe[illegible] Plano Emergency, he was dead by 5:30 A.M. the following mo[illegible]

One half of the Two Bs was dead, and Bruce was very upset. He became withdrawn, and more and more depressed about the freak accident. He would quote a Pink Floyd song to his friends, and say he would see Bill again "some sunny day." The day after Bill's funeral, Bruce decided to make good on his words. After work, turning into the Carrio driveway, Bruce's mother was startled to see Bruce's car in their garage, an unusual place for it. Seeing his feet sticking out the back window of his car, she thought at first he had fallen asleep. But something was wrong. The cassette tape player was playing a Pink Floyd song, "Goodbye Cruel World," there was the odor of gasoline fumes, and the motor was still running. Bruce Carrio, sixteen, was pronounced dead of carbon monoxide poisoning that 23 February 1983. Bruce's rootlessness continued after his death. The Carrios told reporters they cremated Bruce because they did not know where to bury him. "Where is home?" they asked painfully.

A mere six days following Bruce's suicide, on 1 March, Glenn Currey, eighteen, killed himself by carbon monoxide poisoning in his parents' garage. Like Bruce and Bill, he too had been a Plano High School student, but was not friendly with them. He had recently broken up with a girlfriend, and friends wondered if this was what had set him off. It was clear, though, that he had patterned his suicide closely after Bruce's, even down to having music playing as he died of asphyxiation.

The town was in shock, and community action groups were formed, but the suicides continued. On 18 April, Henri Doriot, fifteen, shot himself with a .22 caliber rifle. Pinned to his bulletin board were news items about the Two Bs' deaths, and a sketch labeled "The Ghost of Death." Meanwhile, more than a dozen other young people had attempted to commit suicide since Bruce's death. The methods were as different as the youths attempting, and included everything from a young male who tried to use his own shirt to hang himself, to a young female who sliced up her chest with a pair of scissors.

Soon, the national media turned its attention to the cluster of suicides in Plano. During the week of 15 August 1983, a national newsmagazine did a major story on the growing Texas city and its wave of teen deaths. The spotlight was on Plano's adolescents. Tragically, within a week, three more Plano teens would be dead from suicides.

On 17 August, Mary Bridget and John Gundlah, both seventeen, died of carbon monoxide poisoning while sitting in a car in a garage of a house under construction. They left a suicide note explaining they had been under pressure to break up, but had decided they would rather die than end their relationship. Soon after the Bridget-Gundlah suicide pact, Scott Difiglia, eighteen, apparently depressed over the loss of a girlfriend, shot himself on 22 August, with a .22 caliber rifle. He died the next day at Plano's Presbyterian Hospital. This concentrated series of three suicides in a week, after receiving national media notice, was followed by a long break in suicides.

For whatever reason, almost a year to the day after Bill Ramsey's death and Bruce Carrio's suicide, Plano recorded another cluster death. On 13 February 1984, David Eugene Harris, fourteen, friendly and bright, a computer whiz, came home to parents who loved him, put their .357 Magnum to his head, and killed himself. The only thing his father could figure out that might have been bothering David were his new braces. His death was Plano's seventh suicide in a year. Perhaps it was the anniversary phenomenon at work, where the tragic remembrance of a loss on its yearly anniversary calls forth action, sometimes similar action.

In Plano, the eighth youth suicide occurred on 12 May 1984. Then twenty-two suicide-free months passed, until 23 February 1986, on the exact anniversary of Bruce Carrio's suicide. On that date, an eighteen-year-old senior, who had previously attempted suicide, died of carbon monoxide poisoning. Once again, the flag at Plano High School flew at half mast, and the teens at the shopping center and TTO scratched their heads. They whispered questions about why death had visited them again.

The adults in the community responded with funding and organized efforts at prevention. A twenty-four-hour hotline and a community crisis center now exist in Plano. Guidance counselors were added at the elementary school level, and student groups such as SWAT, Students Working All Together, and BIONIC, Believe It Or Not I Care, were set up. Police officers hold regular office hours in the schools, meeting casually with anyone who wants to talk.

Although the mystery of Plano's cluster remains, some have ventured insights. One Plano family therapist, Glenn Weimer, tends toward the contagion theory in explaining the series of suicides: "I had an adolescent group in the other day, and the kids all agreed that if the first suicide hadn't occurred, the others wouldn't have either. I think they are probably right."

Clear Lake, Texas

The city of Clear Lake, Texas, near Houston, was the setting for another recent suicide cluster. The community of nearly forty thousand is the site of the Johnson Space Center, and until the early 1980s, it was truly a space-age boomtown. But those days have gone. The 1986 deaths of the seven space shuttle Challenger astronauts cast a pall over the city, as it had throughout the rest of the nation. But its tragic precursor, six teen suicides, had visited Clear Lake earlier, in 1984.

In that year, on 9 August, the chain of suicides began when Warren Paul Kuns, nineteen, shot himself in the head while he sat in his car. Kuns was the first of three friends, all high school dropouts, to kill himself. Six weeks later on 17 September, his buddy, Sean Woods, nineteen, shot himself in his pickup truck. At the time, Woods was moving his possessions out of his parents' home. Woods reportedly believed in reincarnation and felt he could return. Soon after Woods's death, another nineteen-year-old friend, Wesley Tiedt, hanged himself from the top of the stairs at his home. A fourth nineteen-year-old friend of Kuns, Woods, and Tiedt was under psychiatric care during mid-October 1984. He was present at Woods's suicide, and told police he had formed a pact with the others to kill himself.

During the week after Tiedt's suicide on 4 October, three other teens beyond the Kuns-Woods-Tiedt circle of friends would take their lives. On Saturday, 6 October, Lisa Schatz, fifteen, killed herself. On Tuesday, 9 October, Gary Schivers, sixteen, hanged himself in his parents' garage. And finally on Thursday, 11 October, ninth-grader Darren Thibodeaux, fourteen, shoved towels under the closed doors of his family's garage, turned on the engine of the family car, crouched next to the exhaust pipe, and died. His seventeen-year-old sister discovered his body lying behind the car. While young Darren was dying that Thursday afternoon, a team of psychologists were counseling students at nearby Clear Lake High School, and Gary Schivers was being buried.

Needless to say, the community was alarmed by the deaths, and feared more. Rumors were circulating that perhaps as many as twenty to thirty teens in the school district might be in a suicide pact. But the police and school officials were trying to dispel such talk.

On Monday night, 15 October, psychologist Dr. Rion Hart met with five hundred parents at Clear Lake High School. He told them that he thought the wave of suicides may have run its course, but warned them not to let their guard down. Some angry parents shouted that they thought the school's hard grading system might be putting pressure on the teens. But not everyone believed this to be true. One senior, Paul Kinze, eighteen, rose and told the audience he felt it was not "drugs, grades, or girlfriends" that was to blame for the deaths, but a "lack of communication between parents and kids."

The last that was heard from Clear Lake, Texas, was that three psychologists were added to the five already on the school district's staff. High school counselors were being trained to look for the warning signs of suicidal risk, and training for junior high personnel was in the works. The suicide cluster of Clear Lake apparently ended.

Death in Suburbia: Westchester, Rockland, and Putnam Counties, New York

PEEKSKILL, NEW YORK, peacefully sits at the end of a narrow valley, on hills that slope abruptly down to the shore line of the Hudson River. These hills are white, and a local joke is to talk of the "white cliffs of Peekskill." But living in Peekskill is no joke. One of the poorest cities in wealthy Westchester County, the community lives in the shadow of the Indian Point Nuclear Power Plant, and recently had the misfortune of being picked to host the area's massive recycling facility.

Even its name sounds difficult and violent—Peekskill. Actually, the city takes its name from Peek's (more properly *Peeck's*) Kill, the creek that runs along its northern borders named for Jan Peeck.

Described as "surprisingly rural" as recently as the 1940s, Peekskill has been transformed into one of those decaying metro-suburban retreats for those employed in the Greater New York City area. The city still tries to retain some of its countryside charm, despite its urban evolution. In the center of Peekskill, for example, there is Chauncey M. Depew Park. An attorney and businessman, Depew was born there in 1834. By 1885, he was the President of Cornelius Vanderbilt's New York Central Railroad. In 1899, Depew was elected to the United States Senate, and gained a reputation for his oratory. The park was seen as an appropriate tribute, as Depew enjoyed appearing in public and liked large gatherings. Depew Park in Peekskill figured in the beginning of a suicide cluster that was to shake the sleepy suburbs of New York City to their foundations. Before the cluster was over, if in fact it is, adults were reexamining their lives and relationships with their children.

The New York cluster started innocently with a boy playing in Depew Park. On 4 February 1984, Robert DeLaValliere, thirteen, went to the park, but instead of playing softball as he usually did, remained distant and isolated from others there. Slowly, he disappeared into the more wooded area. As the sun sank over the horizon, he threw a hemp rope over the branches of a robust tree and hanged himself.

The death was a mystery. DeLaValliere had had no history of mental problems. He had scores of friends and was liked by many at Peekskill Middle School, where he was a seventh-grader. But maybe the warning signs were there? Two weeks before the suicide, educators noticed he had been having trouble in school—missed classes, academic difficulties, and fights with other students. These things were not typical of a boy who had done well in school and enjoyed going to the movies with his friends. One movie he had recently seen that some said made a big impression on him was *An Officer and a Gentleman*. A character that DeLaValliere seemed to have liked a great deal was a young navy cadet who hangs himself in a motel bathroom. Local police openly commented that they thought DeLaValliere may have been imitating the cadet. Friends said he strongly identified with the character. Commented Lieutenant James Nelson of the Peekskill Police Department: "You worry how the violence on television and in movies is affecting young people today, whether the music of today is too suggestive, and what role that might be playing on vulnerable kids."

Did one imitative youth then get imitated by another? Ten days after DeLaValliere's suicide, fourteen-year-old Justin Spoonhour picked a tree in back of his home and hanged himself. Spoonhour lived in Putnam Valley, five miles south of where DeLaValliere died. His mother graphically described in a *People* magazine article how she found her boy. "I turned my light on and saw Justin hanging from a tree," she wrote. "His eyes and mouth were open, and his tongue was swollen and protruding."

Once again, parents and townspeople were shocked. Justin

Spoonhour was not your typical teenager. He was quiet and reserved. He liked classical music instead of popular rock. He acted in Shakespearean plays as opposed to playing with video games. He dreamed of competing in the Olympics in archery, and of singing in the spring choral where he was to do a solo. Justin's mother, Anne, decided to talk to the media to let other parents know that sometimes the warning signs are not clear-cut. "A kid who's talking about which summer camp he's going to attend and what he wants as a graduation present doesn't sound like your suicide type," she noted. "This was a child who was thinking ahead to the Olympics. There's no sense of mortality in that."

But there was something going on inside Justin. Teased by some of his classmates about his interest in the arts, he frequently was angered by the ridicule. But he was a sensitive boy who would not express his feelings. Anne Spoonhour noted he was reserved and often kept things hidden deeply. She said he preferred to avoid confrontations. She wondered about all of this, as she looked for clues as to why he committed suicide. She did not blame Justin's classmates. Not having many friends, being isolated, and closer to adults, he just did not fit in. Observing that the day Justin killed himself was the fourteenth of February, Valentine's Day, his mother speculated as to whether her son felt he had nobody to love.

Anne Spoonhour spoke and wrote a great deal about her boy. She missed him intensely and did not want other mothers to have to go through what she did. "It's very much quieter," she noted. "There's an empty space." All she could hope was that something could be learned from his death, and the suicides might stop.

But the cluster month of February was not yet over. In nearby North Tarrytown, nineteen-year-old James Pellechi, using a shotgun, killed himself at his home on 16 February. A week after Justin's hanging, on 21 February, Christopher G. Ruggiero, seventeen, hanged himself in his bedroom closet with his own bathrobe belt. Funny rumors began to fly about this death. Some said that he had really been experimenting with a form of masturbation. Others were certain it was suicide. The son of the Pelham Village fire chief of ten years, he was the youngest of seven children. Perhaps he felt a need to achieve, for the five-foot, eleven-inch, 160-pound star athlete was called the "best player" on the high school hockey team by Coach Ralph Merigliano. Right before his death, however, something seemed amiss in his life. He had been kicked off the team for a year by the Westchester Interscholastic Hockey League, as the result of an argument with an official during a game. Some friends directly linked that event and his suicide.

On 24 February, Arnold Caputo, nineteen, a very popular and bright Fordham University student, hanged himself from a beam in the attic of his parents' quarter-million-dollar home. He was an excellent musician, and his band had just cut a new demo. But he was going into a slump; rejected by better-known rock groups, he got depressed. The day before he died, he told a friend that he could not take it anymore, but this coded message went unheard. One of his final requests was that when he died, he wanted to be buried with his guitar.

Brian Hart, nineteen, was the youngest of six children, and lived in Bedford Hills. But sometime before 14 March, he drove several miles to Oakwood Cemetery in Mount Kisco, attached a tube to the exhaust, and carried the fumes into the car. Police said he could have been dead for more than a day when he was found.

People pondering the suicides recalled that during 1983, a North Salem seventeen-year-old boy had hanged himself three weeks after his girlfriend had killed herself. They had quarrelled at a drive-in. Did it have anything to do with the 1984 suicides? No one knew.

Through the spring and summer of 1984, Westchester County's teen suicides continued, despite the best efforts of prevention programs and extra hours of counseling. And the suicides had a familiar ring to them. The hanging scene from *An Officer and a Gentleman* seemed to haunt the first of these suicides, and continued to be imitated in many of the following. For example, late in July 1984, Sean Scarborough, twenty, of Yorktown, hanged himself from a tree in the backyard of his family's Sherman Court home.

By fall, school officials in Westchester County had targeted prevention programs for sixteen of the forty-three high schools. Rockland County started similar ones in nine of their high schools. Over twelve hospitals and mental health clinics started support groups. Students, parents, and teachers were lectured by experts on the warning signs of suicide. But the suicides continued.

During the early evening of 11 September 1984, Maureen Fitzell, fifteen, a high school sophomore, walked a quarter of a mile behind her family's Mahopac house, and shot herself with her father's .22 rifle. Reportedly, she was the eleventh youth between thirteen and twenty in Westchester, Rockland, and Putnam counties to have killed herself that year. On 4 October, another sophomore, Nancy McCarthy, fifteen, also killed herself behind her family's home. McCarthy burned to death in Lattingtown, Nassau County, when she apparently doused herself with rubbing alcohol, nail polish remover, and gasoline. Her parents, Dr. John McCarthy, a psychologist, and Egleand McCarthy, a business executive, were at work at the time.

As the year came to a close, the suicides of young people in the three counties persisted. Thirteen-year-old Steven Perro was discovered by his mother, hanging in the attic of their New Rochelle home on 17 October. He left notes saying he was saddened by all the family problems. Eighteen-year-old Robert Valentine was found by his sister at about 7 P.M. on December 20 in the living room of their Haverstraw home. He had killed himself with a gunshot from a high-powered rifle to the head. Two days later, a twenty-one-year-old Mahopac man hanged himself from a basement stairway. John Billingham was discovered by his roommate.

Since 1984, news of the youth suicides of Westchester, Rockland, and Putnam counties has been scarce. In fact, the papers have been more concerned with the numerous reports of UFOs seen over Westchester County. Has the cluster ended, or merely the reporting of the deaths? There are hints that the three counties' problems are not entirely behind them. On 10 February 1985, in response to the public concern about teen suicide clusters like New York's, ABC-TV broadcast the made-for-television movie, *Surviving*. It is the story of a boy and girl who commit suicide by carbon monoxide poisoning. Two days after it aired, Tarrytown, New York, seventeen-year-old David Balogh died in his car of carbon monoxide poisoning. The senior at Sleepy Hollow High School was found at a nearby landfill, and officials noted his was the first suicide in 1985 since the wave of deaths in 1984. David had watched the TV movie, and his friends reported he said he thought it was "really good," and then he had gotten "totally obsessed about it." His father was in a rage and seriously talked about suing ABC. But the stories about young Balogh merely faded away.

During the first week in August 1986, local New York media mentioned that a young man had been found dead in a high school in Westchester County. Apparently, the youth broke into the school, took off all his clothes, and hanged himself.

The events unfolding in the three counties just north of New York City may or may not be over. As with all of these clusters, only time will tell.

"Goodbye Cruel World": Leominster, Massachusetts

LEOMINSTER'S PAST is filled with some proud manufacturing milestones. By 1845, some two dozen factories produced plastic combs in Leominster. Before 1935, seventy-five percent of the piano cases in the United States were made in the north-central Massachusetts town. But in the mid-1930s, the Depression began to take a toll on the city's industries. The days of plants turning out such diverse products as furniture, toys, buttons, fabrics, wool yarn, and paper boxes were over. Today, with a population of over thirty-five thousand, Leominster is a close-knit, blue-collar town that has seen better times. Foster Grant, the sunglasses people, decided to pull up stakes and go to Mexico. Other manufacturers have made similar choices.

And recently the teens started killing themselves. In May 1984, two teenage boys deliberately crashed their car into a loading dock. In the next few months, one youth killed himself while playing Russian roulette, another was killed by a friend with a gun, and yet another was slain in a shooting. Additionally, one teenager was struck and killed by a train. The word around town was that a majority of these deaths were suicides, but at the time the police were treating most of them as accidents.

Suicidologists had long ago speculated that the reported suicides were only the tip of the iceberg, and that many accidents were really suicides. In 1938, in the book *Man Against Himself*, Karl Menninger pointed out that individuals who exhibit dangerously self-destructive behaviors may unconsciously want to kill themselves without taking responsibility for their own suicides. Norman Tabachnick published in 1973 his similar ideas in a book whose title says it all, *Accident or Suicide?: Destruction by Automobile.* And in the same year the Leominster cluster began, one of this country's foremost authors on teen suicides, Richard H. Seiden, Director of Research Programs, Suicide Prevention, and Crisis Intervention of Alameda County, wrote that "suicides tend to be underrecorded because of the social, legal, religious, and economic stigma that still attaches to self-destruction."

The CBS-TV movie *Silence of the Heart* gave a graphic representation of just such an incident in which a teen boy committed suicide, which was at first labeled an accident. Two days after this movie was nationally broadcast, Leominster experienced an event that would no longer let it deny it was in the midst of a teen suicide cluster.

On the morning of 1 November 1984, two 15-year-old girls slipped out of school unnoticed, drank a bottle of champagne, wrote notes of apology for what they were about to do, and then killed themselves. Melissa Christine Poirier and Melody Maillet, sophomores at Leominster High School, were found in Melissa's bedroom. Each girl had been shot once. A .12 gauge shotgun used for skeet shooting was nearby. Melissa's mother, Mariette, had come home for lunch, opened Melissa's bedroom door to let a kitten out, and discovered the tragic scene. Scrawled in lipstick on a mirror was a message from Melissa saying she loved her parents and did not want them to be sad. The girls wrote that their parents should not blame themselves "because we found the gun because if it wasn't that we would have used something else."

Their note also said: "Life sucks and then you die. Goodbye cruel world I'm leaving you now and thier's nothin [sic] you can say to make me change my mind! I love to die. I'd be happier I know it! So please let me go. No hard feelings." On Friday, the day after their deaths, classmates wept openly in the halls of Leominster High School. The school held a moment of silence among its seventeen hundred students, and anxious parents flooded the office with calls to check to see if their children were in school. One teacher had to throw out a test he gave the class on Friday because everyone was in shock.

Since September 1984, Melissa had been depressed. She had gotten into a fight with two girls over a boy, and received a black eye and fractured nose. She was afraid to go outside, and would spend long hours looking out windows. In October, she went to counseling to try to get over her sense of dread. It *seemed* to help. The day before Melissa killed herself, her mother noticed she was happier, did not want to go see her therapist the next day. She even brought home a kitty. Before leaving school the day of the suicides, Melissa had turned in a science project. Science teacher Mark Siemaszko said, "She seemed in a good mood, compared with the mood she had been in."

Months later Mariette Poirier would understand this shift in mood. Often a suicidal person becomes quite perky right before they kill themselves, as they have a firm plan in mind and thus experience a sense of relief and euphoria. That appeared to be what Melissa was showing the day before she died.

Leominster was thrown into the national spotlight. The Sunday following the girls' suicides, headlines in newspapers blared that the community was "stunned" by a "rash of teen suicides." The town was becalmed and awestruck by the events. Hundreds of students attended and mourned the two girls at their funerals, and one teacher said the deaths had a marked effect on some of their classmates. "They grew up a lot, matured a lot, took things more seriously," said science teacher Siemaszko.

Five months after Mariette Poirier found the bodies of her daughter Melissa and Melissa's friend, Melody, she joined forces with Susan Warner-Roy, a neighbor whose husband had hanged himself, to draft a state bill that would put suicide education in public schools. They also raised money for day-long seminars on suicide at the junior high school and guest lecturers on suicide for public forums. Every Tuesday, Mariette Poirier held a counseling group for teens in her living room.

After the girls' suicides, no teens killed themselves for almost a year, despite several attempts. Then in October 1985, a fifteen-year-old boy shot himself. John P. Finn was found in the hallway of a friend's home with a single bullet wound in his head and a .38 caliber handgun lying near his body. Determined that this death not attract the attention the others had, School Superintendent Louis Amadio immediately closed all junior and senior high schools to the media. "Sudden death is not the school's responsibility but a community awareness problem. Everybody has to be more aware of problems confronting teens these days," Amadio said.

Finn's best friend was William J. Lovetro, seventeen. A few minutes before 1986 officially began, Bill Lovetro died. He killed himself by ramming his car into the concrete foundation of a factory.

Disturbed by the suicides, Leominster Mayor Richard Girouard called a meeting at the city hall auditorium, and asked the town's students to attend. Only about twenty-five came. Then two Boston television crews showed up. The crowd was angry at the media for their stories about Leominster and its suicides, and let them know it. And the students were frustrated with the tired old answers when the mayor brought up drugs as if it was one of the reasons behind the deaths. They pointed instead to competition with friends and to pressures in school and at home. The more they talked, though, the more everyone realized that no one knew why any of the adolescents had committed suicide.

Mental health counselors were by now having weekly sessions at Leominster High to deal with the feelings that were sweeping through the school. On Thursday, 27 March 1986, they opened their session a little differently with a surprise announcement. Speaking to the entire student body, they told everyone there that the night before George Henderson, fourteen, a freshman honor student, computer whiz, and member of the school's cross-country track team had killed himself. The students and their teachers then observed a moment of silence. Guidance counselor Patricia Pothier said, "The kids are just amazed and shocked by this. They like the boy very much and they don't understand why [he killed himself]."

Diane M. Henderson had discovered her son's body in his bedroom when she returned home from work shortly before 6 P.M. The family's .12 gauge shotgun was at his side. He had died from a self-inflicted wound to the head. One neighbor said, "They were just an everyday, normal family. The family did everything together. They went canoeing. They went mountain climbing. You name it. They did it together."

"With every new one it gets more baffling," Mayor Girouard said after George's death. "This boy was a total surprise. He was an honor student with no apparent problems. Just a nice kid." The mayor said officials had been keeping an eye on some students who were having difficulties, but the Henderson boy was not among them. "Neither was the last young man who killed himself," Girouard said. "We were watching his friend, but not him. . . . It's gotten to the point where many of the kids are saying 'If they want to kill themselves, let them go ahead and do it. It has nothing to do with me,' and it's very difficult to get past that attitude," the mayor observed.

Susan Warner-Roy, in the meantime, noted the problems were not going away. She had heard about fifty attempted suicides in the last six months, and was deeply concerned by the latest incident. School and town officials said they had tried to prevent future suicides but were unclear why their effort had failed. "We just don't know why," noted Leominster High Principal George J. Antonioi. "We've tried a lot of things, but obviously we haven't hit on the right combination." The publicity had been difficult for the students, though, he knew that, and he flatly refused to allow reporters to interview students. As one student put it, "Why can't they just leave it alone? We are not freaks." Two days after the death of George Henderson, as they had done before, guidance counselors visited homerooms. Then school went into recess on Good Friday, and many took the day to ponder the recent suicides.

As the new growth of spring moved into the rolling countryside around Leominster, town officials brainstormed new ideas to address the wave of suicides. Guest lecturers from the Centers for Disease Control were brought in. Mariette Poirier and Susan Warner-Roy's group, SPACE, Suicide Prevention Awareness Community Education, got fuller backing. A Leominster Youth Committee was formed. Numbering almost twenty members, including students, doctors, parents, public officials, clergy, and businessmen, the Youth Committee was brought together to tackle the difficult situation at hand. "Somebody has got to do something," said Carolyn Barney, Community Relations Director at Leominster Hospital, and member of the new committee. "I think this stands a chance of doing something positive. I don't think we're going to wipe out all the problems, but we're sure going to make a stab at handling as many of them as we can."

Leominster School Superintendent Amadio made a phone call to Larry D. Guinn, Director of Student Services in Plano, Texas, and asked for help. "It felt good to talk to and share information with someone else who has gone through it," Amadio said after his hour-long conversation. "What I like about the Plano approach is it doesn't focus on any kind of course called suicide prevention, but focuses on teenage stresses and self-esteem. And they emphasize how it's a community problem, not a school problem."

Early in June 1986, as the school year wound down, things seemed to be returning to normal. People were stepping back and trying to assess the events of the previous two years. The Massachusetts School Counselors Association acknowledged the great amount of work being done in Leominster High School. Guidance counselor Patricia R. Pothier was honored and cited by the association for her organization of counseling sessions for students needing to cope with Leominster's suicides.

But then on 18 June, shock came again. A twenty-year-old man who had moved to Leominster only a month before was found in his car, dead from a self-inflicted gunshot wound to his head. Michael Dionne had moved from the nearby town of Ashburnham. Police responded when a local resident reported he had heard a gunshot. They found Dionne in his car in the middle of the road. The car's engine was running, its lights on. Next to the young man's body was a rifle.

Police Chief Alan Gallagher said he was "making no connection" between Dionne's suicide and those of the teens. But others, locally, were wondering: Do people move here just to kill themselves? The remark spoke to the limbo in which people in Leominster still found themselves. And another question was raised, as it had been at similar cluster sites: Would there be more youth suicides?

These two questions were soon answered with a bizarre suicide in September of 1986. A young man from Concord, New Hampshire, chose Leominster as the site of his suicide, and he seems to have imitated one of the first teen suicides in the cluster in fulfilling his death wish. Like the two teenage boys who smashed their car into a loading dock, this young man from New Hampshire died by crashing his auto into a concrete wall at a shopping center. This latest suicide in Leominster left city officials scratching their heads and wondering what they could do about their town's strange magnetism which appeared to pull the potentially suicidal to its borders.

Native American Clusters

Manitoulin Island, Ontario

THE LOCATION was an isolated farmhouse on a fifty-mile-long northern Ontario Indian Reservation. The date was Christmas Day 1974. A seventeen-year-old boy, disturbed by the forthcoming separation of his parents, drank a large amount of alcohol, and then took a .22 caliber rifle and fired a bullet into his own head. He died some eight hours later.

Within a year in the small rural community of just thirty-seven families on Manitoulin Island, eight other youths were dead. The city of Little Current sent over their coroner John F. Bailey, and the Native Mental Health Service dispatched counselor Joseph Fox. Along with psychiatrist J. A. Ward, the team discovered the following facts about the tragic chain of suicides: Ranging in age from seventeen to thirty-one, suicide victims averaged twenty-two years of age. Five of the nine were male, and all were single. Six used guns as their method. Six killed themselves at or near their parents' homes. Except for one suicide, drinking was involved in the deaths. All had "a negative sense or absence of self-esteem. . . . All of the victims showed a striking absence of any intimacy in their interpersonal relationships," wrote Ward and Fox.

The research into this cluster showed that the rate of suicide for that reservation for the one year of this series was 267 per one hundred thousand, an astronomical rate compared, for example, to the United States rate of twelve per hundred thousand for suicides. Ward and Fox concluded that the "series of suicides indicate a true suicide epidemic."

Suicidologists have found that Native Americans in general, and some tribal groups in particular, have had extremely high rates of suicide. In Alberta, for example, Menno Boldt of the University of Lethbridge found that from 1976 to 1982 young Indian males were killing themselves at a rate that was twenty to thirty times the Canadian average. And psychiatrist James Shore noted that some American tribal groups have suicide rates ten times greater than the general population. What has surprised many researchers is the extremely large pockets, or clusters, of Indian suicides taking place.

Duck Valley, Nevada

Alan Berman, while a professor at American University in Washington, D.C., did a study of the Duck Valley Indian Reservation in Nevada, and found the isolated spot had the highest suicide rate in the United States. Berman discovered that from 1949 to 1980, the reservation's population of twelve hundred had experienced fifty suicides. These numbers translate into a rate of 150 per hundred thousand.

Berman said the Shoshone and Paiute of Duck Valley have as much an alcoholism problem as other reservations, but the isolation of the reservation contributed to the higher incidence of suicides. Duck Valley's Bureau of Indian Affairs officer, James Formea, put it this way: "I'm not sure it's any different than living on the outside. It's isolated without a doubt. It's a hundred miles to a city on both sides. There's no recreation. If you're not adept at entertaining yourself, you go absolutely bananas."

Wind River, Wyoming

The general isolation, alcoholism, high unemployment, and despair found on the reservations of many native North Americans seemed to be an underlying cause for one of the largest suicide clusters in recent years, that of Wyoming's Wind River Reservation in 1985. The deaths began on 12 August, when Reynold Wallowingbull, twenty, used his socks to hang himself in the Riverton City Jail. He was in jail after having been arrested for intoxication.

On 16 August, Donovan Blackburn, sixteen, a popular student at St. Stephens School, hanged himself from a tree with his sweatpants. Teachers remembered him as one of the brightest students, and an outstanding athlete. Four days later a close friend, Darren Shakespeare, fourteen, was found hanging by baling wire from a tree. He had been at Blackburn's wake, and threatened he would be next.

The fourth suicide was Paul Dewey, twenty-three, who hanged himself on 13 September. The next day, Edwin Norah, twenty-two, was found hanged, and four days after that Thomas Littleshield, nineteen, hanged himself in the Riverton City Jail. Roderick Underwood, fourteen, was the seventh suicide, and Levi Trumbull, twenty-four, who hanged himself on 28 September, was the eighth. Two days later, a twenty-five year old man hanged himself in a closet of his home. He used the drawstring from his sweatshirt. His sister discovered his body. Eight of the suicides were Arapaho and one was a Shoshone.

On 1 October, Salt Lake City television news reporter John Harrington and his cameraman Wayne Paige flew into the Wind River Reservation to report on the suicides. "Unbeknownst to them, the night before a ninth suicide victim had been found and feelings were fairly hostile," their news director John Edwards said. They had done some reservation interviews, and then driven to the St. Stephens cemetery to shoot some outtakes on videotape. Although the graveyard looked deserted, as they set up their equipment, five carloads of Indians suddenly appeared. Before they knew it, the newsmen were looking down the barrels of several shotguns. Soon, their cameras were smashed and their videotapes burned. Over forty thousand dollars worth of equipment was destroyed. After some tense moments, the KTVX men were permitted to pack up the rest of their stuff, and told to hightail it.

After the incident, tribal elders and leaders held a news conference to warn the media not to intrude on the grief felt by many of the reservation's families. Many clergy, school, and mental health officials announced they would answer no more questions from reporters. Counselors who have lived on the reservation all their lives had never seen such a crisis. They noted that since the beginning of the year, over fifty youths, including two young women in recent weeks, had attempted suicide. Yet another community was looking for answers to its suicide cluster.

"We don't have any reasons, and we're pretty frustrated," said Fremont County Coroner Larry Lee. "It's tragic. They haven't even lived and they kill themselves." Father Tony Short, a Jesuit priest at St. Stephens Mission, noted, "Indians have tremendous feelings. Anyone who thinks they're stoic is wrong. They have a lot of feelings that they keep inside and are not dealing with. People think liquor can loosen them up, but the problem is alcohol is not neutral." He also noted among the suicide victims that "many come from extremely troubled homes."

Marjene Tower, a behavioral specialist with the Bureau of Indian Affairs, felt the suicides were "some sort of contagion that we don't understand. I've never seen this kind of epidemic before." Tower's most shocking discovery was the fact that all of the fourteen- to seventeen-year-old suicide victims were best friends, pallbearers at each others' funerals. Among the young men, they were all "drinking buddies." She felt the suicides were "caught" like other diseases spread among closely related individuals.

Coroner Lee could not say if the deaths were linked. "Some of them were friends," he observed. "Some of them have attended the others' wakes. But they're all single suicides. As to the connection, I don't know if there is. It's just a domino effect." Obviously, Lee is talking about the behavior contagion of the suicides, but appears to be denying this in his statement, instead holding out for the prominent single suicide notion.

Suicide prevention sessions were held weekly in the area schools during the fall of 1985, and students openly discussed the lack of recreational resources and presence of alcohol on the reservation.

On 7 October, the community's Arapaho youth took part in a sacred tribal ritual, which had in the past been used to ward off illness. The ceremony had been last performed in 1918, when the tribe was faced with an outbreak of Spanish influenza. Near the tribal sun dance ground four feathers, each with a red ribbon attached and each blessed with the Arapaho sacred pipe, marked the points of the compass to cleanse any unhappiness that might have prompted the suicides. Inside a tepee on the grounds, a tribal elder cleansed about a dozen members of the tribe at a time by tapping on the ground, painting each face with sacred red paint, and having them step over a burning herb. Hundreds of the reservation's students stood in lines outside the tepee, waiting to go before the elder. After the ceremony allowed the youth to rediscover and rekindle their traditional ways and identity together, Wind River was calm. During the winter of 1985 to 1986, the ancient ceremony and a modern task force of agencies delivering family counseling seemed to have worked; no suicides took place.

On 18 March, as spring began to warm the Wyoming air, an eighteen-year-old Arapaho youth hanged himself. He became Wind River's tenth suicide since its cluster began. Dismayed, tribal leaders attempted not to dwell on the suicides and to address positive issues. As Danice Romersa-Kulia, director of the Shoshone-Arapaho Indian Children Welfare program put it, "We have to look forward. You can't always be looking over your shoulder at the past." Still, at Wind River and other reservations across the country, suicide prevention workers, community leaders, and parents wonder if another outbreak is just a season away.

A Week in February:
Omaha, Nebraska

ONE OF THE most recent nationally publicized suicide clusters occurred in Omaha, Nebraska. Like the cluster of 1983 in Texas and the 1984 cluster in New York, Omaha's 1986 chain of suicides began in February. Over a five-day period, three students from Bryan High School killed themselves. The four-grade, 1,250-student high school is located on the outskirts of Omaha, in a white, working-class neighborhood. According to reports from their families and friends, the three did not know each other very well, but the quick succession of their deaths made everyone ask questions about the contagious nature of suicides among teens.

Michele M. Money, sixteen, died first, on 3 February. School counselor Nancy Bednar said she "was a very pleasant girl. She wanted to be a counselor. She had a sensitive side." But the product of a broken home, depressed over problems with her boyfriend, and struggling with the decision of whether to stay in school, she overdosed on her mother's Elavil, an antidepressant. In the past, friends had recalled they thought she was always positive about things.

Next was Mark E. Walpus, fifteen. Like Michele, he came from a broken home. He was a popular guy who spent his last winter working alone in his shop. Everyone thought he was on the way to college. Instead, he fired a bullet into his chest the day after Michele died. A suicide note was discovered.

Thomas E. Wacha IV, eighteen, was described as a fairly quiet loner who was deciding whether he really wanted to go to trade school. He had recently told a friend he was "disgusted with life." Captain Dick Mackley of the Sarpy County Sheriff's Department reported that on the morning of 7 February, Tom had been involved in an automobile accident, and fought with his parents. That night Tom died from a self-inflicted shotgun blast to his head.

Four other Bryan High students had made serious attempts on their lives. On 26 January, a seventeen-year-old male had slashed his wrists and lived. Another fifteen-year-old boy had taken a drug overdose on 5 February and survived. The others had made similar tries.

As had happened before in other parts of the country, the community responded with sympathy and support. At Bryan, an emotional pep rally was held with the theme, "Choose Life." Students wore yellow "We Care at Bryan" buttons and heart-shaped "Choose Life" stickers. Cheerleaders and bands performed and students linked arms and sang "We Are the World" during the hour-long event. Although Bryan was labeled "Suicide High" by some in Omaha, in general the community tried to lend assistance. Burke and North High School students took huge banners to the pep rally to show their support for the high school. Principals from ten schools in West Omaha sent 108 dozen donuts to Bryan. Joslyn School principal Sandra Pistone said, "We all want Bryan students to know that this is not just their problem. We're all in this together." Intensive counseling sessions were held for students and parents. Each homeroom teacher asked their students to pledge: "I will not make any big decisions, especially decisions concerning my health, safety, life and the feelings of my loved ones, without taking a day think it over."

However, anger soon surfaced as well. At a public forum, parents and other adults shouted down psychiatrist John Florian Riedler with comments about the lack of help in past times of need. Some Bryan students interrupted Riedler, accusing him of talking over their heads, and asked why teens had to die before help became available. Rumbings about "shutting the barn door after the horses have got out" were heard.

One of the first to jump in was Russell Walpus, twenty, a Bryan graduate. "My brother was Mark Walpus, the one who died on Tuesday. The kids don't understand what you're trying to get to. It doesn't make any sense to them."

"We all do the best we can," Riedler told the overflow crowd packed into the school's six-hundred-seat auditorium. He added that he understood there was "a lot of anger" in the school. Riedler told the media: "Hysteria swept over this part of town last week. We're dealing with a confused bunch of people who are going through the regular stages of grieving."

Television reporters and other news media members combed the school hallways, interviewing students and peering into classrooms. Many students criticized the presence of television news crews. Press coverage began with a small Associated Press story on 9 February, and by 11 February, Omaha's suicide cluster had been featured in such papers as the *New York Times*, the *Boston Globe*, and *USA Today*. On Wednesday, 12 February, ABC's "Nightline" devoted a segment to Omaha's wave of teen suicides. United Press International and Associated Press wire services ran stories through 13 February.

"It's kind of upsetting to know that you get publicity for this kind of thing and not for something good like a good basketball team," said Kathy Stone, fifteen, the student council vice president.

The council's president, Dave Jeck, eighteen, observed: "I don't think that these suicides can be related specifically to our area. These suicides were caused by the same thing that causes every other suicide. They were depressed." Jeck also said, "The first one may have set off the others. It may have put the idea in their heads that that is the way out."

School district psychologist Donna Chaney said, "Everybody involved—including the students—wants us all to get back to normal. Part of what we need to do is to restore calm."

By the middle of February, things were returning to normal, and various parts of the community that had been criticized were being seen in a new light. Local ABC affiliate KETV assisted in helping a suicidal youth get some help. The student, whose name was not released, left a desperate-sounding message on a teacher's answering machine. KETV made a plea for that specific student to call Omaha's Personal Crisis Hotline, and spent the day broadcasting the telephone number. The student finally did dial the number and got help. Al Krumprey, director of the Personal Crisis Hotline, said their phones had been "ringing off the hook." Krumprey commented,

"The suicides affect all of us here. They affect the psyche of the city."

As that February ended in Omaha, calm was returning to the city. But people wondered, why a suicide cluster and why here? Barbara Wheeler, a member of the American Association of Suicidology, former director of Mental Health at Bergen Mercy Hospital, and a crisis hotline trainer, summed up what a good many local folks were thinking. Although the three suicide victims had separate friends, different hobbies, and different Bryan High School activities, she noted their deaths may not be unrelated. The death of one teenager may have been seen as a solution by the others. Wheeler concluded, "Suicide is the ultimate form of communication."

In the Wake of Omaha?: Spencer, Massachusetts

EARLY IN February 1986, Omaha was hit by three student suicides. Starting on 9 February, the rest of the country was hit with a barrage of wire service and broadcast media stories on Omaha's suicide cluster. Beginning on that same date, Spencer, Massachusetts, was pulled into a vortex of teen suicide and suicide attempts. Before the month was over, one adolescent was dead by suicide, and eighteen others had made twenty-five attempts on their lives.

Spencer is a town of eleven thousand, lost in the central part of Massachusetts, not far from the big city of Worcester. Forty miles north is Leominster, well known for its suicide cluster of recent years. Spencer formerly had been a manufacturing town, involved in shoemaking since 1811, and was famed as the birthplace of Elias Howe, Jr., the inventor of the lock-stitch sewing machine. In 1986, it became known for its cluster of suicide attempts.

According to Police Chief Robert A. Parker, Jr., two of the early attempts were made on Sunday, 9 February. At about 4 P.M., a young igh school freshman, fifteen, slashed her wrists. That night around ne, a sophomore boy, sixteen, drank iodine. Both were rushed to hospitals and recovered. Both were students at David Prouty School in Spencer.

On the next day, Prouty junior and football player, sixteen-year-old Francis V. McNamara, shot himself with a .22 caliber rifle in the second-floor bathroom of his Old Farm Road home. The next morning, Tuesday, he died at Worcester City Hospital. "I was shocked, because he was a super boy," said Diana Hart, thirty-nine, whose four sons played Little League baseball with Frank McNamara.

"I just couldn't believe it. I didn't think anybody at the school would do it," commented sophomore Rick Arsenault, fifteen. He noted the football tight end hadn't appeared to be troubled, but then "Frank wouldn't be the type to tell you what his problems were."

On the day Frank died, Superintendent of Schools Philip F. Devaux met with the students of the 750-pupil high school. Devaux announced that guidance offices and some classrooms would be open Tuesday through Friday of the following vacation week to give troubled students someone with whom to talk. He told the students that representatives from Tri-Link, a social service agency from Southbridge, would be available during the school vacation for parents as well as students. "We emphasized to them the need to communicate their feelings with their parents, school counselors, their peers, and teachers. For the remainder of the school week all school district energies will center on assisting the students," Devaux said, "who have lost a classmate and a friend."

On the day after the assembly, counseling groups were set up at Prouty High School. Rumors had begun to circulate that as many as three other students had tried to kill themselves Monday night, and school officials were worried. Certain questions, however, were being raised about the actions of school officials. Counselors from Tri-Link had advised against the assembly. Psychologist Pamela Cantor, then the president of the American Association of Suicidology, warned against encouraging a large turnout at the funeral. "In that way, a kid with no importance becomes important through death," she said. "Kids copy that." She cautioned that organizing the entire school to attend a funeral has not helped in previous cases. "Such a funeral is not about a celebrity event. It's about the death of a kid who made a tragic choice."

On Thursday, 13 February, more than two hundred parents and adults crowded into the cafeteria of David Prouty High School to discuss the recent events. Most expressed anger and upset over the media coverage of the story. As the parents' meeting was held, students conducted another meeting elsewhere in the school that was off limits to the press.

At the adults' meeting, school band director George Garber said Boston television stations had been aggressive in drawing comments from some high school students. Garber noted that the stations had never before reported positive stories from Spencer. The gathered crowd applauded his comments at length. Superintendent Devaux said that while some reporters had acted professionally, others had not. Tri-Link staff noted that while some Boston media had intensified the teens' problems, other local media had handled the events sensitively. Devaux also expressed dismay at the fact that communication was so poor with the police, and some parents were concerned that no town officials had chosen to come to the meeting.

The social service staff from Tri-Link went into action soon after being invited to help. As they assisted the students and parents, they began to discover the true extent of the cluster of suicide attempts. They found that the first attempt had actually occurred in December 1985, when a fourteen-year-old girl had tried to kill herself. Then in January 1986, two seventeen-year-old girls attempted suicide. By the end of March, eighteen students had made twenty-five suicidal attempts, with five youths being hospitalized for a month. The methods used included guns, iodine, nail polish remover, pills, hanging, and cutting.

Soon, a strong network of friends was detected by mapping the relationships between the students who had made suicide attempts in Spencer's junior high school and high school. The friendship bond among them was extremely strong, but the interactions that held them together were generally negative. Making a suicidal attempt was seen as one way to retain membership in the group. A number of high school students seemed to be linked to the junior high crowd who were friends of the fourteen-year-old who had attempted suicide in December. Tri-Link's positive intervention lasted six weeks at the school and turned a grave picture around. After they left, programs they had set up continued and succeeded in giving individual attention to still-troubled teens.

Concern for teenagers in Spencer was high after the crisis waned. In March, Teen Action was formed. Anita L. Crevier said her idea for the group was born in the aftermath of young Frank McNamara's suicide. She told of how her daughter had comforted Frank's girlfriend after his death and expressed the notion that others could benefit from simply getting together. This prompted them to call ten friends to a meeting in their home. From this initial session came the idea to form Teen Action. Meeting twice a week at the

Spencer Senior Center on Main Street, discussions of the group would center on the adolescents' problems, and each member would suggest alternatives to suicide as a solution to the teens' concerns. Through basic problem-solving, Teen Action tried to get at the root of the town's suicides.

Teen Action has been behind other projects as well. They have a question-and-answer column in the local paper and on a Worcester radio station. The group sponsored their first dance early in April. Teen Action is also backing an effort to have teenagers added to the town boards as nonvoting members. Anita Crevier said many teenagers feel their needs and concerns are not considered when public officials discuss issues that may affect their lives.

The 11th of the Month Club: Mankato, Minnesota

SITUATED IN southwestern Minnesota, Mankato is a city of some thirty thousand individuals. The town got its name from the Sioux word for the blue earth found in the vicinity. Nestled in the Blue Earth River Valley, the lay of the land has had a lot to do with the future of Mankato. The two-hundred-foot-deep valley dictated that the streets run from northeast to southwest, paralleling the terraces of the sharp slope. The side streets then had to be constructed with a steep grade.

On 6 February 1852, three St. Paul men began building the town of Mankato after buying the land from Sioux chief Sleepy Eye. The uprising of four-hundred Sioux in 1862 produced one of Mankato's major footnotes in history. Of the hundreds tried, all but thirty-eight were pardoned by Abraham Lincoln. The simultaneous hanging of those thirty-eight Sioux is the largest legal execution that has ever taken place in the United States. You can still find a granite marker on the site of the execution, at the northwest corner of Front and Main streets.

Another form of mass death has recently visited the town. In 1986, Mankato became the site of a cluster of suicides which one newspaper reported was "Minnesota's largest in memory." Interestingly, people in the area began to take note of it only during the same week Omaha was getting all the attention for their rash of suicides. In Mankato, on 11 February, young Diane Lamont had taken her own life, and folks grew concerned.

But Mankato's brush with teen suicide had begun a month earlier. Bryan Javens, 18, shot himself to death in his bedroom on 11 January. A champion wrestler and three-wheel racer, Javens was a senior at Mankato East High School. Not much was made about Bryan's death, but it did receive a small write-up in a local paper. The report on his suicide was pinned to the headboard of Diane Lamont's bed. The fifteen-year-old Mankato East sophomore killed herself the same way Bryan had. She shot herself in her bed. Police officials said they knew each other.

The Mankato suicides prompted local authorities to call two public forums. One was attended by three hundred people, and another by eight hundred. Mankato's citizens were upset. Experts on teen suicide discussed warning signs, officials tried to restore calm, but in general most residents were unsatisfied.

Then something weird happened on Valentine's Day. Unknown persons got the community access cable television station to broadcast a message to Bryan Javens and Diane Lamont. The video valentine addressed to the pair read:

Hope you are having fun.
Glad you're together.
We miss you.
Love,
East High

Blue Earth County Sheriff LaRoy Wiebold was outraged. He had the station pull the Valentine's Day message after he received a report that a copycat suicide pact had been formed by other teens. CCTV Channel 13 had to shut down for two hours to remove the video, and some townspeople complained the sheriff had violated the First Amendment. Others were happy with his actions, and thought he might be on to something. The suicide pact report the sheriff had obtained was about the "11th of the Month Club." Rumors were circulating that another Mankato East student would commit suicide on 11 March. Sheriff Wiebold said he had "an intelligence report on the possibility of a copycat pact being formed by other young people."

Meanwhile, Mankato Mayor Herbert Mocol said that stories

were going around "that there's going to be a suicide on the eleventh of each month. We've heard it again and again."

Kimberly Evers, twenty, did not wait for the eleventh. On 19 February, she died of carbon monoxide poisoning in her family's garage. She was one of four children and had graduated from Mankato West High School in 1983. People said she had known Bryan Javens and Diane Lamont. Employed at fast-food restaurants in Mankato, Kimberly had graduated in December 1985 from a Minneapolis school for travel agents. Her boyfriend of three years, Tim Scheitel, was shocked by her death. They had planned to marry.

When the morning of 12 March came, there was a general sigh of relief that another suicide had not taken place. But when the *Mankato Free Press* decided to print an article reporting on the relief of the students and their families, the newspaper office was flooded with angry and concerned phone calls. One of them was from Audre Scheitel, mother of seventeen-year-old junior Tim.

From information at the public forums, Tim Scheitel's mother knew he was a prime candidate for suicide, because of Kimberly's suicide. Thus she just did not like the tone of the article. Tim's father noted that Tim's friends "did everything imaginable. They lined him up with girls, took him to parties. But what do you do when your young people deal with death? It's a pain so strong it can be all-consuming. You tell them you love them and you tell them there's a God and that's the best you can do."

On 26 April 1986, Tim was alone at home except for his eleven-year-old sister, Jessica. Their father, a rock musician, and their mother were at a Saturday night gig outside of Mankato. Early in the evening, Tim went into the garage, left the door closed, and started the car. Thinking he might be trying to kill himself the same way his girlfriend had, Jessica told Tim she was sick. He turned off the car, and stayed with his sister until he put her to bed at 10 P.M. Then Tim Scheitel went back to the garage. His body was found on Sunday morning by his parents. He had died of carbon monoxide poisoning.

After Tim's suicide, a change seemed to come over Mankato. Len Zimmerman, principal of Mankato East High School, said there would be no large assembly. "We've been told by psychologists that we shouldn't talk about it because the more publicity there is, the more chance you get the copycat effect," he said. The town was left with a feeling closely akin to that expressed by Sheriff Wiebold: "There are no answers. There are just questions."

After Tim Scheitel's suicide, there was a long calm in Mankato, but then late in 1986, another East High student committed suicide. Early on 25 November, a sixteen-year-old junior was found hanged at her Mankato home. The young girl was the fifth youth suicide in Mankato, the fourth from the 940-student high school in one year. Police officials and high school personnel refused to comment on the latest suicide, saying they believed that publicity might prompt other suicides.

Part 3

"With man, most of his misfortunes are occasioned by man."
—Pliny the Elder,
first century A.D.

Conclusions of the Cluster Investigators

SOON AFTER THE waves of suicide clusters were noticed by the public and the media in the early 1980s, a new type of suicidologist appeared: the suicide cluster researcher. Needless to say, these investigators have had little time to complete their in-depth studies in such remote locations as Plano, Texas, and Mankato, Minnesota. Still, sought out by reporters, school officials, and grieving parents, this new breed of researcher has been forced to answer innumerable questions on a subject about which little information is available. Their replies give us insights into their current thinking and the theories in the field.

Psychologist David Clark of the Center for Suicide Research and Prevention and director at Rush-Presbyterian-St. Luke's Medical Center in Chicago is studying suicide clusters under a grant from the National Institute of Mental Health. He has been looking into the Chicago area clusters for some time. "There is clearly a contagion factor," he said in May of 1986. "Kids who are depressed and sitting on the fence don't need much of a nudge. The suicide death of one young person makes it easier for the next one." And how widespread is the phenomenon of suicide clusters? "All of us who are interested in clusters know of several that exist for every one that is reported by the media," Clark said.

Lucy Davidson, a physician with the Centers for Disease Control in Atlanta, is one of the most widely quoted suicide cluster researchers in America. At CDC she has access to data on many outbreaks. Working along with Mark Rosenberg and Patrick O'Carroll of CDC and Madelyn Gould of Columbia University she is deeply involved in suicide cluster research. "We're just trying to put together a statistical methodology for studying cluster suicides and finding out some of their characteristics," says Davidson. "One of the difficulties is that there are no statistics on clusters and little information available outside of news reports."

Davidson has warned that mass assemblies and media blitzes following a suicide may inadvertently tip the balance causing another troubled teen to see an individual problem in larger terms. "They begin to think that maybe if they did it, it will have an impact and will be noticed," Davidson commented in April 1986. "People think rationally most of the time, but not so rationally when thinking about suicide. They think they'll be around to watch the community react, and they don't really appreciate that they'll be dead."

For the towns and areas hit with a series of suicides, Davidson believes there is no magic formula. "Sometimes things happen, in a positive sense, that change the community, and there are no suicides for a long period. On the other extreme, on the negative side, maybe all those likely to commit suicide have done so, and another won't happen for a while. We would hope we could all work for the positive to happen," she said.

One of Davidson's colleagues, Patrick O'Carroll, an epidemic intelligence service researcher at CDC, often comes to conclusions that seem different from those made by Clark and Davidson. Appearing before a group of civic leaders in Leominster, Massachusetts, in May of 1986, O'Carroll said there is no evidence that media coverage of teen suicides leads to more of the same. "There's no hard evidence that more publicity makes it worse. There's worry in a number of circles that in 'clusters' of suicides, not just youth suicides, that if there is a 'contagion,' that the way it is spread is through information. But whether the press increases this knowledge or if everyone is already aware of it is still an open question," he said.

Asked directly about the series of teen suicides in Leominster, O'Carroll replied: "It sounds to me that they were suicides that occurred close to the same period of time and it seems there were more than we would expect. But I'm not sure that I'd put them together as a cluster." O'Carroll suggested the Leominster teen suicides were nothing more than isolated incidents. "We don't know what percentage of youth suicides occur in group clusters, but we think it is very small," O'Carroll said.

Mark Rosenberg's definition of what makes up a suicide cluster was quoted in the introduction to this book. To restate briefly, they are groups of deaths, closely related in time and space, having at least three or more completed suicides, and were often of young white males. "You don't want to panic people by using words like epidemic and contagion," Rosenberg noted. Realistically, however, he felt suicides, like other forms of violence, spread like wildfire, from person to person in our country. "You have to wonder if exposure to a first suicide triggers the later deaths in these kinds of clusters," he said.

Meanwhile, at Columbia University, David Shaffer, chief of child psychiatry, and Madelyn Gould, associate professor, are also studying clusters. During the New York series of 1984, Shaffer said he felt imitation could be a factor in the adolescent suicides. He thought the large community meetings may be "responsible for at least the secondary wave that characterizes these outbreaks. The meeting highlights and gives status to the behavior and lowers the threshold for vulnerable kids who otherwise wouldn't have engaged in suicide," he said. He found that many young suicide attempters had reported recent personal contact with another suicidal adolescent. He encouraged communities to prevent the news from reaching the media and to avoid mentioning it in schools.

Looking at the suicides in New York, Gould gave some of her findings at the 1986 Annual Meeting of the American Association of Suicidology. She said: "In Westchester, in examining whether or not the youths even knew each other, it turned out that none of them did know each other, which leads us to think there can be indirect transmission of contagion, perhaps through the media, which was the common link, at least, in that cluster."

Alan Berman, psychologist and past president of the American Association of Suicidology, noted after the Omaha series, "The first [suicide] serves as a model for other vulnerable individuals."

Douglas Jacobs, an assistant professor of Psychiatry at Harvard Medical School and Director of the Cambridge Hospital Center for the Study of Suicide, speaking about Leominster, said of clusters in general: "We know that it happens in all kinds of communities, but we don't know why it happens in one community and not another." At the time of the Spencer crisis, Jacobs told officials there something similar. "A particular town doesn't have to throw up its hands and say we've got this horrible problem. It can happen to any town," he said.

Jacobs also noted, "There does seem to be a contagion effect, like the wave in a football stadium. But it's like AIDS—more research needs to be done."

After a series of murder-suicides in British Columbia and Alberta within a two-week period during September 1986, forensic psychiatrist Herbert Pascoe feared the cluster was not coincidental. "I'm sure there is a copycat factor. It's unusual to have so many in such a short period of time. It's pretty uncommon, and all of a sudden we have three in Western Canada," Pascoe said. Donald Milliken, director of Alberta Hospital's Forensic Services, agreed. "There may be a possibility of copycatting going on," Milliken said, adding that the area needs further study.

In general, most of the individuals on the front line of suicide cluster research agree that contagion is a factor in the clusters, although they do not know its extent. Beyond that, the answers to the phenomenon are not readily apparent, and the search continues.

The Media and Contagion

WHAT INFLUENCE do the media have on suicide clusters? Throughout the 1980s, this question has been asked frequently by parents and local officials attempting to deal with the notion of contagion and imitation in teen suicides. Research has been conducted along this line of inquiry, and the survey results plus some pointed stories give insights into this area of conjecture. Let us first turn to an early suicide cluster incident that illustrates this notion of popular culture affecting a series of self-inflicted deaths.

The Werther Effect

In 1774, Johann Wolfgang von Goethe, who today is most often remembered for his work, *Faust*, wrote a novel entitled *The Sorrows of Young Werther*, in which the central character commits suicide. The book was the rage of Europe, and soon afterward people claimed many suicides were completed in imitation of Werther's. As Goethe observed, at first a handful of individuals transformed "poetry into reality" and shot themselves. "What occurred at first among a few took place later among the general public," Goethe commented at the time.

Afraid of the spread of this suicide cluster, governments in Italy, Denmark, and Germany banned the book. Authorities in Copenhagen would not let it be published. Officials in Milan purchased all copies and destroyed them. But the lessons from Goethe's work were mostly forgotten for two hundred years.

Then in 1974, sociologist David P. Phillips of the University of California at San Diego examined suicide statistics in relationship to suicides publicized in newspapers, and found a significant increase after a front-page suicide. "It seems appropriate to call this increase in suicides 'the Werther effect,' after Goethe's hero," wrote Phillips. He went on to say he felt "this effect is probably due to the influence of suggestion." Phillips's evidence is convincing. He found, for example, in an admittedly extreme American incident that after Marilyn Monroe's suicide, which was front-page news throughout the nation, the United States suicide rate briefly increased by twelve percent—197 people more than normally would have, killed themselves in the month after Monroe's suicide. Indeed, of the thirty-three well-publicized U.S. suicides that Phillips studied, he found a significant rise in the national suicide rate after twenty-six of them occurred.

Phillips is the foremost researcher in America now looking into this whole issue of the media, imitation, suggestion, and suicide. In 1983 he was awarded the prestigious Socio-Psychological Prize from the American Association for the Advancement of Science in recognition of his work. In 1977 and 1979, Phillips published his study relating an increase in automobile fatalities to well-publicized suicides. He showed that in the state of California, when a front-page suicide story was carried in the *Los Angeles Times*, the *San Francisco Chronicle*, or other dailies, the number of auto accident deaths increased three days later by thirty-one percent, and by over nine percent in the week after the suicide. The more publicity the suicide got, the more the increase in motor vehicle deaths. Additionally he found that most of these accidents were single car crashes, leading him to speculate that some may really be imitative suicides.

Murder-Suicides

Phillips followed these findings with his discovery that after a well-publicized murder-suicide, there is an increase in private, business, and corporate aircraft accidents. Here, too, he found that the greater the mass media attention to the suicides, the greater the increase in the number of plane crash fatalities. He theorized that the murder-suicide stories might be triggering imitative murder-suicides, which were disguised as airplane accidents.

Anecdotally, one can watch these kinds of trends in the newspapers and broadcast news. For example, on the Friday afternoon of 16 May 1986, former police officer David Young and his wife Dorris took over the Cokeville (Wyoming) Elementary School, and held 150 students and teachers hostage. Reportedly, the siege ended when one of the Youngs' homemade gasoline bombs went off, killing Dorris, and burning scores of fleeing, screaming children. At this point, David Young turned his Colt .45 on himself.

This nationally broadcast suicidal event was followed by the killing that night of five people at a bar and nearby convenience store in Colorado Springs, Colorado, by plumber Gilbert Eugenio Archibeque. Cornered by police, Archibeque shot himself once in the head with his .237 caliber handgun at 2 A.M., Sunday morning, 18 May 1986.

From Friday, 16 May, through Sunday, 18 May, the news media dwelled on the deaths, murders, near-murders, and suicides in the western states of Wyoming and Colorado. These front-page stories, if we read Phillips correctly, would then lead to some disguised suicides soon afterward. It seems they may have. On Monday, 19 May, newspapers such as the *Washington Post* and the *New York Times* as well as the major wire services noted that the weekend had been one of the bloodiest in recent history in terms of small private plane crashes. Seventeen people had died and seven were injured in noncommercial aircraft accidents in New Jersey, Georgia, Oregon, Indiana, and California. Meanwhile, in Temecula, California, two other folks had died in a hot air balloon crash that left a third occupant critically injured. Were Phillips's insights correct?

After killing fourteen postal workers in Edmond, Oklahoma, on Wednesday, 20 August 1986, Patrick Sherrill turned a gun on himself. This tragic event is another recent example of a well-publicized murder-suicide having a possible immediate effect. According to police investigators in Knoxville, Tennessee, Suheil "Sam" Obeid killed twelve-year-old Matthew Holbert as the two watched television that Wednesday night. Obeid then turned the gun on himself. The police speculated that the broadcast news of the Oklahoma massacre had directly influenced Obeid.

Such stories and accounts, however, do not convince social scientists; but the statistical work of Phillips and others is bringing the connections between these life-and-death events to a high level of analysis, which cannot be easily disputed. And Phillips's survey results have uncovered some very interesting details of the effect of the media on future events.

TV News and Suicides

After Phillips's early work, he began to examine the impact of television on suicides, and later other forms of violence. In 1982, he and colleague Kenneth A. Bollen of Dartmouth published the results of their work showing that suicides definitely increased after, not before, a national news story of a suicide. They found that with news stories of suicides, there was an imitative peak of suicides the day of the story, the day after, and on days six and seven following the broadcast. With motor vehicle fatalities and airplane accidents, the peaks were on days three and eight following the publicized suicides. They felt the different peaks may relate to the difference between overt suicides, and the covert ones disguised as car or plane accidents. Straightforward imitations of the publicized suicides came quickly, whereas the more hidden, indecisive suicides took a bit more time to take place.

In September of 1986, David Phillips and colleague Lundie L. Carstensen had their study, "Clustering of Teenage Suicides After Television News Stories About Suicide," published in *The New England Journal of Medicine.* Looking at 12,585 teen suicides and thirty-eight suicide news stories from 1973 to 1979, they found these youth suicides increased significantly in the week after the broadcasts, especially among girls. They concluded that the best explanation for the phenomenon was that the television news stories actually "triggered" the additional suicides of the teens. The publication of this article (and the companion one by Madelyn Gould and David Shaffer; see the section titled "*Surviving*" in this chapter) started a debate among suicidologists and news executives as to the true extent of the effect of the media. In an editorial in the same issue of *The New England Journal of Medicine,* Dr. Leon Eisenberg said: "It is timely to ask whether there are measures that should be undertaken to limit media coverage of suicide."

In rebuttal, CBS's George Schweitzer felt it would be "ridiculous and irresponsible to ignore issues like teenage suicide." Charlotte Ross, director of the Youth Suicide National Center said: "What we're looking for is not suppressing coverage of teenage suicide but increasing it. I also think it's possible for these studies themselves to have a negative impact, if what they do is frighten the public into being scared of addressing the issue."

Interviewed soon after the article was published, David Phillips observed: "It is really up to the news media themselves to decide where it leaves us. Only the media should be involved in the debate.

"As a native of South Africa, a country without freedom of the press as we know it, I value freedom of the press very highly. I would be very upset if people used my findings in order to suppress news media coverage. But I do think it would be responsible for the news media themselves to bear in mind results of studies like these."

Soap Operas and Suicides

Extending some of his earlier work to fictional television stories, Phillips also correlated suicides in soap operas to a rise in the rates of suicides, motor vehicle deaths, and near-fatal accidents. Phillips's 1982 paper on the subject was the first systematic evidence that these television programs trigger deaths as well as near-fatal accidents in the United States today.

During 1986, researchers in England discovered that Phillips's work on soap operas also rang true in that country. In the week after 2 March, when a suicide attempt was shown on the British Broadcasting Company's program, "The Easterners," suicide attempts increased. For example, at an East London hospital, where seven overdoses per week were the average, twenty-two cases were reported. So many new cases came in that temporary beds had to be set up. Writing in the medical journal *The Lancet*, Hackney Hospital doctors Simon Ellis and Susan Walsh wrote, "Do the BBC programmers consider the likely consequences of screening self-destructive behaviour that is likely to be copied? Next time, could they please arrange for Angie to take an overdose in the summer when our bed state is not so acute?"

By extending Phillips's general research, are there any specific cases we can examine to see if there is something going on here, in relation to teen suicides and clusters? Adolescents, by the time they graduate from high school, will have been exposed to eighteen thousand murders and eight-hundred suicides on television. For a population of individuals who watch, on the average, eighteen to twenty-eight hours of TV per week, the impact of television is great. On 16 October 1974, when a Kaiserlautern, Germany, youth of nineteen killed himself after watching the movie *The Exorcist,* some serious attention was directed toward the impact of such movies. But it has been only in recent years that more systematic studies have occurred, especially regarding movies broadcast on television. Two important examples of this mix of cinema and TV that have been analyzed are the movies *The Deer Hunter* and *Surviving.*

The Deer Hunter

Has the televising of the movie *The Deer Hunter* served as a model for some suicides? Certain researchers, including Thomas Radecki and Alan Berman, indicate this may be the case. In one of the movie's scenes, the characters played by Robert DeNiro, Christopher Walken, and others are forced by Vietnamese Communists to play Russian roulette. Later, Walken's character becomes so distraught by his memories of the war that he plays willingly and kills himself.

Dr. Thomas Radecki noted that after television stations and videotape rental use of *The Deer Hunter,* some viewers were committing suicide by playing the deadly game. He called for an editing of the broadcast version of the film. But little heed was taken. For example, Donald Bouley, twenty-three, of Andover, Minnesota, shot himself in the head during a game of Russian roulette inspired by watching the movie *The Deer Hunter* on television, according to the Anoka County Sheriff's Department. Witnesses reported that Bouley had been drinking the night of 13 June 1981, at a party at his apartment. He and several of his friends viewed an uncut version of the movie. Bouley then put a pistol to his head, pulled the trigger once, and killed himself with the gun's only .38 caliber slug.

Early in November 1981, Radecki had asked Chicago station WFLD-TV to edit the Russian roulette scene before they showed *The Deer Hunter.* Radecki told the station that twenty-eight shootings and twenty-five confirmed Russian roulette deaths in the United States involved people watching the movie on videotapes or television. The movie was broadcast uncut despite his warnings. On Saturday, 21 November 1981, two male viewers shot themselves to death after watching the film. In separate incidents, David Radnis, twenty-eight, and Ted Tolwinski, twenty-six, both of the Chicago area, sat down at their kitchen tables, held partially loaded guns to their heads, and pulled the triggers. By March 1986, Berman and Radecki had documented forty-three Russian roulette deaths worldwide since 1978 attributed to imitations initiated by watching *The Deer Hunter*. (See Appendix for a complete list.)

Interestingly, the whole concept of Russian roulette may have developed out of suicide cluster activity. In Meerloo's book, *Suicide and Mass Suicide*, he wrote that eighteenth-century Russia was noted for its religious sects who devoted most of their energies to suicides. "Their self-killing in shifts, by coincidence, is still known as Russian roulette," observed Meerloo.

Surviving

On 10 February 1985, due in great measure to the massive public interest in teen suicide clusters like those in Texas and New York, ABC-TV broadcast the made-for-television movie, *Surviving*. This extremely well-made drama starred the actor Zach Galligan and the rising young star Molly Ringwald. The story of a teen couple who die from carbon monoxide poisoning, it shows the actual suicides, then the effects the deaths have on their families.

Did the movie have a contagious effect on teens? Were some suicides in some way caused by the broadcast? As noted in the section on the New York series, two days after it aired, seventeen-year-old David Balogh of Tarrytown died in his car of carbon monoxide poisoning. The Sleepy Hollow High School senior had watched the movie, and his friends reported he said he thought it "was really good," and that he had gotten totally "obsessed about it." David's father directly blamed the film.

In the midst of a suicide cluster in Jefferson County, Colorado, the mother of another suicide victim felt the movie had a concrete impact on her daughter. Marcia Wenger noted that shortly before her daughter Keri killed herself, she had watched *Surviving*. "The first hour showed the kids and their deaths, and the last hour was about the families and the devastation the death caused. Keri sat there enthralled with the first hour, but she tuned out the second hour totally. She was fascinated with the death and with the kids. I think it was almost like her life. It was giving her the okay," Marcia Wenger noted. She pointed out further that Keri left her suicide note in the 18 February 1985 issue of *People* magazine which featured a cover story, complete with color photographs of Ringwald and Galligan, on *Surviving* and teen suicides. Marcia Wenger openly wondered if the movie played a key role in her daughter's suicidal decision.

Madelyn Gould of Columbia University, one of this nation's foremost suicide cluster researchers along with her colleague, Dr. David Shaffer, did a study of the effect of the made-for-television movies on completed youth suicides in the metropolitan New York area, all of New Jersey, and southwestern Connecticut, and on admitted attempters at six New York area hospitals. Using what they called the natural experiment of four television movies involving teens and suicide broadcast between October 1984 and February 1985, Gould and Shaffer developed a complete suicide register. During their twenty-five-week observation period, they recorded 220 suicide attempts and thirty-one completed suicides. In the two-week period following the movies, by doing a rigid statistical analysis, they anticipated sixty-two attempts. What they found were eighty-eight attempts. Statistically, what was expected in terms of completed suicides after the movies were six deaths. They found thirteen completed suicide deaths—an extra seven suicides. As Gould said during a conference in 1985: "That's a significant increase."

Epidemiologist Gould calculated that these deaths were in excess of the normal rate, as the overall suicide rate was less before and after the effect produced by the movie. Projecting to a national level, she felt that there may have possibly been eighty excess deaths of ten- to nineteen-year olds, in some way related to the showing of the movies.

Writing in *The New England Journal of Medicine,* Gould and Shaffer concluded that "television broadcasts of fictional stories featuring suicidal behavior may in some cases lead to imitative suicidal behavior among teenagers. . . . The presumptive evidence suggests that fictional presentations of suicide may have a lethal effect."

Certainly the showing of *Surviving* is a case in point. After the broadcast, for example, doctors and nurses at a community hospital in Waterbury, Connecticut, noted a sharp increase in suicide attempters. Writing in the *American Journal of Psychiatry*, Ostroff, Behrends, Lee, and Oliphant stated that two days after the movie, a boy and girl were admitted who had attempted a suicide pact as in *Surviving*. By the end of two weeks, fourteen teenagers had tried to kill themselves, had been discovered, and rushed to the hospital.

This fourteen in half a month was compared to the usual two to four cases *per month*.

Alan Berman of American University decided to conduct a national survey of the impact of *Surviving*. He collected data from nine urban medical examiners' offices in Atlanta, Cleveland, Dallas, Ft. Lauderdale, Philadelphia, San Diego, Seattle, St. Louis, and Washington, D.C. While Berman did not find an overall increase in total or teen suicides, he discovered a "noticeable shift in the proportion of youth suicides by carbon monoxide." As this was the mode of suicide in *Surviving*, Berman felt the "shift might be accounted for by a process of identification and imitation."

But basically, Berman came away from his study not believing the movie caused new suicides. "There is a suggestion that there was an imitative effect only in the shift of method chosen by youth who otherwise were known to be suicidal before the movie aired," he told the National Conference on Prevention and Interventions in Youth Suicide in June 1986.

Clusters and the Media

If a "hot story" about a cluster is receiving a great amount of national press and television time, as happened during February 1986 with the Omaha series, then other stories will usually appear with a clusterlike framework soon thereafter. This occurred during February 1986 with the Spencer, Massachusetts, and Mankato, Minnesota, suicides. Suicide clusters appear to demonstrate the Werther effect: one teen suicide suggests another, and so on, within a community, or even the same high school. Some teen suicide clusters have occurred exclusively among students at one high school. For example, six of the Montana teen suicides committed in 1985 were current or former Capital High School students, and fifteen of the adolescent suicides since 1981 were current or former students of that one high school.

Teen suicide clusters in 1986 have followed this same trend. In Omaha, Nebraska, where three teenagers died between 3 and 7 February, and two others made attempts between 26 January and 5 February, all were Bryan High School students. Meanwhile, in Spencer, Massachusetts, between 9 and 13 February, four publicized attempts (there were over two dozen unpublicized ones) and one completed suicide occurred; all were students at David Prouty High School.

Did the publicity surrounding the Omaha, Nebraska, series have a direct influence on the other American teens? The reports began with wire service stories from Omaha, dated 9 February, and continued through the *USA Today* and *New York Times* treatments of 11 February. The series in Spencer really began in earnest only after the publicity from Omaha. Elsewhere, similar things occurred. On 11 February, a fifteen-year-old girl in Mankato, Minnesota, killed herself. Since there was a teen suicide in that same community on 11 January, the local media's attention was heightened during the Omaha series with regard to these two cases. More stories were produced in the Minnesota press regarding the two suicides. Then Mankato's wave saw another, its third suicide only eight days after the flash of the Omaha suicide publicity. As February ended, other incidents were reported, but as the Omaha series began to get less and less press, Spencer and Mankato suicides and attempts dropped off.

Steven Stack, who has extended the work of Phillips, found that highly publicized celebrity deaths, such as Freddie Prinze's, produced higher rates among people the same age and sex as the famed suicides. Since Phillips's and Gould's 1986 studies indicated that suicide stories are not precipitating suicides that would have occurred anyway, but are actually creating additional suicides that would not have happened without the media suicide accounts, we can thus naturally expect the rash of news stories on teen suicide clusters to produce other youthful suicides.

The Werther effect's most logical application today therefore is in the study of teen suicide clusters. The whole issue of suggestion and imitation among adolescents committing suicide is one causing insightful considerations by suicidologists, crisis workers, police, teachers, community leaders, and sociologists. The Werther effect is most manifest in the phenomenon of suicide clusters, and the potential for peaks in suicides after a well-publicized suicide report should not be underestimated.

Music, the Message, and Suicide

DESPITE the overt influence of television, perhaps nothing rules and reflects the culture of adolescents like music. Rock and roll. New Wave. Punk. Heavy Metal. Death Rock. The beat, lyrics, groups, and individual artists are held in high regard. Rock star look-alikes are everywhere. And the fashion follows the music in more than clothing. Attitudes and belief systems are being born from the messages being communicated or reinforced through teen music. What is the place of music in the schema of suicide?

In the recent past, music as a form of mass media has affected people's lives and deaths. The story of "Gloomy Sunday" is a case in point.

Gloomy Sunday

Written in Hungary in 1933 by composer Rezso Seress and lyricist Laszlo Javor, "Gloomy Sunday" enjoyed moderate success and little attention until 1936. In that year, Budapest police found a suicide note containing lyrics from the song near the body of shoemaker Joseph Keller. An immediate investigation by the authorities discovered that a total of eighteen suicides had been inspired by the ballad. Specifically, two persons had committed suicide after hearing it played by a gypsy band, a few killed themselves with the sheet music in their hands, and others committed suicide while listening to recordings of "Gloomy Sunday." Budapest authorities banned the song.

American producers saw a hot property and quickly became interested in the piece. They commissioned Sam M. Lewis (of "Five Foot Two, Eyes of Blue," "I'm Sitting on Top of the World," and "Absence Makes the Heart Grow Fonder" fame) to write the lyrics. By March of 1936, three records, by Henry King, Hal Kemp, and Paul Whiteman, were being promoted as "Gloomy Sunday, the Famous Hungarian Suicide Song."

Soon "Gloomy Sunday" was recorded by famous singers of the time: Billie Holiday, Paul Robeson, Artie Shaw. But its impact in America was not as great as its Hungarian version. The song, telling of a sad mourner whose lover has just died and is thinking of ending it all, apparently caused no suicides in this country, even though its airplay was unrestricted.

As authors Hal Morgan and Kerry Tucker noted in their book *Rumor!*, the song brought wealth but not happiness to its Hungarian composer. "In 1968, at the age of sixty-nine, Reszo Seress committed suicide by leaping from a Budapest building," they wrote.

Suicide Solutions

Suicide themes turn up occasionally in more recent popular music. Simon and Garfunkel's 1965 songs "Richard Cory" and "A Most Peculiar Man" are similar in terms of their despair and loneliness as a source of suicide. Elton John's 1972 "I Think I'm Gonna Kill Myself" speaks frankly to the notion of a teenager's desire to commit suicide, get some publicity, and see who cares about his death. In the 1976 Blue Oyster Cult song "Don't Fear the Reaper," about a proposed suicide pact, suicide is portrayed as a positive choice.

During the early 1980s, one song that became connected to the whole issue of imitation and suggestion by way of music was Ozzy Osbourne's "Suicide Solution." Ozzy, thirty-seven, former leader of the heavy metal group Black Sabbath and known for such outlandish stunts as biting off the head of a bat on stage, found himself in 1986 being sued for causing the suicide of a teenager.

On the evening of 27 October 1984, nineteen-year-old Ozzy Osbourne fan John McCollum of Indio, California, went to his bedroom. There he listened to one of Ozzy's albums containing "Suicide Solution," and killed himself with his father's handgun. Allegedly, he spent five hours listening to "Suicide Solution." The song contains the lines:

Breaking laws, locking doors, but there's no one at home.
Make your bed, rest your head, but you lie there and moan.
Where to hide? Suicide is the only way out.
Don't you know what it's really all about?

McCollum's father filed suit against Ozzy Osbourne and CBS Records early in 1986 in Los Angeles Superior Court, charging that the singer's "violent, morbid and inflammatory music . . . encouraged John McCollum to take his own life."

His mother said, "The police photo shows the headphones were still on when he died."

"They knew this record was going to encourage or promote suicide," said Tom Anderson, the McCollums' attorney. "I think we have in this case opposing forces: Satan and God."

Ozzy claimed he was misunderstood, and that the song was really anti-suicide, anti-drug, and anti-alcohol. His attorney, Howard Weitzman, fresh from winning John DeLorean's case, said the lawsuit was "a slanderous assault on artistic freedom. On this premise, one might equally make a connection between teenage suicide and *Romeo and Juliet*. The logical extension of this type of suit is censorship."

On 7 August 1986, Superior Court Judge John Cole dismissed the suit against Osbourne. The judge said that although the music "may be totally objectionable and repulsive" to many, the McCollums' attorney failed to show why Ozzy's songs should be exempt from First Amendment protection. Judge Cole said, "Trash can be given First Amendment protection, too."

Soon after the Ozzy Osbourne case was dismissed, another music-suicide suit was filed. During December 1986, the British rock group Judas Priest and CBS Records, Inc., were ordered to stand trial in a civil lawsuit that charged them with inducing two Reno, Nevada, teens to shoot themselves. James Vance and Raymond Belknap allegedly formed a suicide pact and shot themselves with a shotgun after spending six hours listening to an album by the band. Belknap died from the December 1985 shooting, while Vance was severely disfigured.

Kenneth McKenna, Belknap's mother's attorney, stated that "the suggestive lyrics combined with the continuous beat and rhythmic, nonchanging intonations of the music combined to induce, encourage, aid, abet, and otherwise mesmerize the plaintiff into believing the answer to life was death."

Meanwhile, lawyers for CBS Records and Judas Priest argued that the band was protected by constitutional guarantees of freedom of expression and insisted that there was no claim in the suit for which the band could be held liable for damages. The Judas Priest music-suicide trial is expected to begin during the fall of 1987.

Rock Stars and Suicides

Rock fans sometimes follow the lead of their idols in fashion, in hairstyle, in behavior, and in suicide. Some of the musicians' suicides have become major news because of the star's status. Recently, the impact of such suicides has been extremely great. In the past, they were often ignored.

According to Dave Marsh and Kevin Stein in their *The Book of Rock Lists*, one of the first noteworthy rock musician suicides was that of Johnny Ace, who died on Christmas Eve 1954, while playing Russian roulette backstage at Houston City Auditorium. More recently, other musician suicides have included Paul Williams of The Temptations in 1973, Pete Ham of Badfinger in 1975, folksinger Phil Ochs in 1976, Donny Hathaway in 1979, and Ian Curtis of Joy Division in 1980. Marsh and Stein also noted the complex suicides of two other famous rockers. Rory Storm, onetime Mersey beat bandleader (Ringo Starr was playing with Storm and his group The Hurricanes when Starr joined The Beatles) was found dead in his home in 1974, with his head in the oven, the result of a suicide pact with his mother, whose body was found nearby. Terry Kath of the group Chicago died at the Los Angeles home of a friend in 1978, when the gun he was playing with, à la Russian roulette, went off as it was pointed at his head. This occurred in full view of his wife and one of the band's sound crew.

Rock stars' nonsuicidal violent deaths sometimes are connected to later self-inflicted deaths. Herbert Hendin, in his *Suicide in America,* wrote: "After John Lennon was murdered, several suicides linked their deaths to his."

The prototypical hero of teen suicides is Sid Vicious. Sid, as a member of The Sex Pistols, foreshadowed much of the new wave and punk rock movement now so well established in America and Europe. Sid Vicious and his girlfriend Nancy Spungen were sad and lonely characters. Late in the 1970s, their pathetic punk love affair turned very dark, and, so the theory goes, they made a murder-suicide pact. In October 1978, Sid stabbed Nancy, killing her. But he did not commit suicide himself until 3 February 1979. This twisted love story is still the source of much examination and groupie interest, especially in New York City. During 1986, the play *Vicious,* the book *And I Don't Want to Live This Life,* and the movie *Sid and Nancy,* were very popular with teen punk rock followers. How much Sid Vicious's suicide influenced the suicides of young people in the metropolitan New York area may never be known, for the impact may be hidden in the covert behaviors, such as drug abuse, that are so much a part of Sid's old Twenty-third Street underground scene.

Some suicide followings are much more obvious. One of the biggest recent clusters, occurring after a popular singer committed suicide, happened in Japan.

Japan's Singing Idol Suicide Wave

On 8 April 1986, at 10 A.M., teen singing idol Yukiko Okada, eighteen, was found with slashed wrists in her gas-filled apartment. Two hours later, she climbed to the top of her seven-story recording studio building and jumped. Despondent over an unhappy love affair with an actor, according to one media account, "old enough to be her father," she had been hospitalized in the days before her leap. Yukiko Okada had not always been so sad. In 1983, she won a national talent contest, which was followed in 1985 by her receiving an award as Japan's top new singer. She was extremely popular and had a great following.

This popularity became even more evident soon after Okada's death. The place that Okada's body hit, a busy downtown Tokyo street corner, became an impromptu shrine where many laid wreaths. Some fans could be seen standing at the corner, gazing upward at the building from which she jumped. The media broadcast several hours of reports on the Okada suicide, interviewing her family, her friends, even the boyfriend who jilted her. But no one knew how influenced her fans were by her suicide until they began killing themselves in a concentrated chain of deaths.

The cluster began two days after Okada's suicide when two sisters, aged twelve and eighteen, jumped from the roof of their apartment house. In the next days, young people, at least one a day, killed themselves in apparent imitation of the Okada suicide. For example, on 16 April, sixteen-year-old Pak Migi told her sister, "I want to become like Yukiko Okada," before plunging from the thirteenth floor of her building.

The newspapers and television stations began spending an enormous amount of time analyzing Okada's and her followers' suicides. One seventeen-year-old high school student Izumi Furukawa noted, "I think [Yukiko Okada's] death triggered this. My friends, we all talked about it after that and said how we've felt like doing it too." The media attention was intense.

The rate of suicides dramatically increased. During the weekend of 19 and 20 April, five young people under eighteen killed themselves, including one girl who was just nine years old. The nine-year-old jumped from the roof of a department store west of Tokyo, after having been scolded by her mother. The girl had told friends she was very affected by the Okada suicide. The same weekend, three others in their twenties did the same thing. On Monday, 21 April, six people under twenty killed themselves. On Tuesday, 22 April, the total for the day was five; one was a fourteen-year-old boy who set himself afire. The next day, a fifteen-year-old Fukuoka City boy hanged himself at a construction site.

Thirty-three young people took their lives in the seventeen days following Okada's suicide. Number thirty-three, on 24 April, was twelve-year-old Tomoko Humaska. She jumped from the thirteenth floor of her suburban high-rise apartment building. She left a note to her parents saying, "I'm sorry it had to end this way." Family members said that the girl had repeatedly replayed and watched a television program about Okada's suicide that had been videotaped.

One of the last suicides in this cluster occurred on 2 May, when twenty-one-year-old Masanno Majima jumped from the same roof as Okada, and landed where her makeshift shrine had been. Majima had photographs of Okada in his pocket, and had been seen loitering in front of the building for several days before his jump. Twenty-two of the thirty-four deaths were like Okada's, suicides by jumping from buildings. The others were by hanging, fire, or asphyxiation.

Midway through the wave of deaths, famous child psychologist Tsutomu Komazaki of Josai University said, "This is definitely a trend. These kids see someone doing it, and they get the same idea. We're seeing a snowball effect here." By mid-April 1985, a total of 177 Japanese under twenty had killed themselves. But by the mid-point of the 1986 Okada suicide cluster, 213 youths had committed suicide, thirty-six more than for the same period the previous year.

Whereas in similar events, some Americans might have been cautious about linking one death with another, there seemed little doubt in the minds of the Japanese that the wave of suicides were directly related to the young singer's death. As the National Police Agency spokesperson declared, "Since she died, we have indeed seen a lot more kids jumping off buildings or killing themselves by other means."

The influence of music and the media appear to be strong on the minds and actions of young people around the world, and suicide clusters seem to be one of the consequences.

Future Note

IN 1897, Emile Durkheim published his classic study of suicide. He was able to analyze suicides in probably the most thoughtful way they had ever been studied until his time. Durkheim's insight—that individual behavior (i.e., suicides) can be fully understood only by referring to the social context in which they occur—has become the foundation of the sociological perspective. He is to be admired for his work.

The legacy of his work haunts the study of suicide clusters. In Durkheim's chapter on imitation, he noted that many suicides would occur in succession, especially in the military. He also observed: "In 1813 in the little village of Saint-Pierre-Monjau, a woman hanged herself from a tree and several others did likewise at a little distance away. Pinel tells of a priest's hanging himself in the neighborhood of Etampes; some days later two others killed themselves and several laymen imitated them. When Lord Castelreagh threw himself into Vesuvius, several of his companions followed his example. The tree of Timon of Athens has become proverbial."

Although Durkheim said "no fact is more readily transmissible by contagion than suicide," he also felt that imitation did not "affect the social suicide-rate," and "its radiating influence is always very restricted." Unfortunately, Durkheim was convinced that the role of behavior contagion had little to do with the wide-ranging spread of suicide. Because he is so highly respected, and is seen by many as one of the most important early sociologists and the grandfather of suicidology, Durkheim's influence has lived long past his lifetime. The study of contagion and clustering has thus suffered.

The time has come for a reawakening of the extremely important exploration of contagion and clustering as critical components in suicide behavior. This book's journey through ancient, historical, and contemporary suicide clusters, into the various insights and theories of the field's researchers and investigators, and among the lives and deaths of many victims, should certainly raise questions in the reader's mind about the epidemic-like effects of the phenomenon. The body of the heretofore isolated incidents of suicide clusters brought together in this work points to a deeper mystery than we could have previously comprehended. Suicides tend to collect in clusters; there seems little doubt about this. But what are the psychological underpinnings of the phenomenon? There are some suggested connections, but few hard answers. And how can we prevent this tendency? These questions are left for future research.

Recently, at a packed end-of-the-season Boston Red Sox baseball game, I experienced a more pleasant form of behavior contagion than we are discussing here, namely the so-called "Wave." Struck by how spontaneously the crowd began and extended this joyous expression, I wondered if there might be some way to tap the sociological and psychological energy being channeled into suicide clusters, and turn the tide in a more positive fashion. It is something I ponder often, as I read about yet another suicide cluster.

APPENDICES

"The man who, in a fit of melancholy, kills himself today, would have wished to live had he waited a week."

—VOLTAIRE, 1764

Appendix One: Teen Suicide Clusters of the 1980s—A Chronology

- 1980–1981—Fairfax County, Virginia—Twenty teen suicides occurred during the school year. Speaking before a congressional hearing in 1984, Marcia and Robert Scherago, a northern Virginia couple, told of their horror at finding their sixteen-year-old son hanging from a backyard tree, a rope around his neck.
- 1980–1981—Larimer County, Colorado—Twelve teens killed themselves in eighteen months.
- 1982—Milwaukee County, Wisconsin—Three youths committed suicide within days of each other.
- August 1982—Cheyenne, Wyoming—Three teens killed themselves.
- 1983—Groveport, Ohio—Over the period of one weekend, three adolescents committed suicide.
- 23 February 1983—Plano, Texas—Bruce Carrio, 16, committed suicide (see text).
- 29 February 1983—Plano, Texas—Glenn Currey, 18, committed suicide (see text).
- 18 April 1983—Plano, Texas—Henri Doriot, 15, committed suicide (see text).

- 17 August 1983—Plano, Texas—Mary Bridgit, 17, and John Gundlah, 17, committed suicide together (see text).
- 22 August 1983—Plano, Texas—Scott Difiglia, 18, committed suicide (see text).
- 1984—Houston, Texas—Twenty-nine people under age twenty killed themselves within six months.
- 1984—Elizabethtown, Pennsylvania—A wave of teen suicides hit the area.
- 1984—Santa Barbara, California—Teen suicide outbreak occurred.
- 4 February 1984—Peekskill, New York—Robert DeLaValliera, 13, committed suicide (see text).
- 13 February 1984—Plano, Texas—David Eugene Harris, 14, committed suicide (see text).
- 14 February 1984—Putnam Valley, New York—Justin Spoonhour, 14, committed suicide (see text).
- 16 February 1984—Tarrytown, New York—James Pellechi, 19, committed suicide (see text).
- 21 February 1984—Pelham Village, New York—Christopher G. Ruggiero, 17, committed suicide (see text).
- 24 February 1984—Fordham, New York—Arnold Caputo, 19, committed suicide (see text).
- 14 March 1984—Mount Kisco, New York—Brian Hart, 19, committed suicide (see text).
- May–October 1984—Leominster, Massachusetts—A total of four teens committed suicide and two others died violently in the early months of this cluster (see text).
- 12 May 1984—Plano, Texas—A local teen committed suicide (see text).
- July 1984—Yorktown, New York—Sean Scarborough, 20, committed suicide (see text).
- 9 August 1984—Clear Lake, Texas—Warren Paul Kuns, 19, committed suicide (see text).
- 11 September 1984—Mahopac, New York—Maureen Fitzell, 15, committed suicide (see text).
- 17 September 1984—Clear Lake, Texas—Sean Woods, 19, committed suicide (see text).
- 4 October 1984—Lattingtown, New York—Nancy McCarthy, 15, committed suicide (see text).
- 4 October 1984—Clear Lake, Texas—Wesley Tiedt, 19, committed suicide (see text).

- 6 October 1984—Clear Lake, Texas—Lisa Schatz, 15, committed suicide (see text).
- 9 October 1984—Clear Lake, Texas—Gary Schivers, 16, committed suicide (see text).
- 11 October 1984—Clear Lake, Texas—Darren Thibodeaux, 14, committed suicide (see text).
- 17 October 1984—New Rochelle, New York—Steven Perro, 13, committed suicide (see text).
- 30 October 1984—CBS-TV aired the made-for-television movie, *Silence of the Heart*, about teen suicides (see text).
- 1 November 1984—Leominster, Massachusetts—Melissa Christine Poirier, 15, and Melody Maillet, 15, committed suicide together (see text).
- 20 December 1984—Haverstraw, New York—Robert Valentine, 18, committed suicide (see text).
- 22 December 1984—Mahopac, New York—John Billingham, 21, committed suicide (see text).
- 1985—Richardson, Texas—Five youths committed suicide over a twelve month period, three of them within three weeks.
- 1985—Brainerd and Crosby, Minnesota—Several teen suicides were noted.
- January 1985–May 1986—Jefferson County, Colorado—Eighteen teens committed suicide. Of these, three were Golden High School students.
- 10 February 1985—ABC-TV aired the made-for-television movie, *Surviving*, about teen suicides (see text).
- 12 February 1985—Tarrytown, New York—David Balogh, 17, committed suicide (see text).
- 18 February 1985—Jefferson County, Colorado—Keri Wenger, 16, committed suicide (see text).
- 12 August 1985—Wind River, Wyoming—Reynold Wallowingbull, 20, committed suicide (see text).
- 16 August 1985—Wind River, Wyoming—Donovan Blackburn, 16, committed suicide (see text).
- 20 August 1985—Wind River, Wyoming—Darren Shakespeare, 14, committed suicide (see text).
- 13 September 1985—Wind River, Wyoming—Paul Dewey, 23, committed suicide (see text).
- 14 September 1985—Wind River, Wyoming—Edwin Norah, 22, committed suicide (see text).

- 18 September 1985—Wind River, Wyoming—Thomas Littleshield, 19, committed suicide, and soon afterward so did Roderick Underwood, 14 (see text).
- 28 September 1985—Wind River, Wyoming—Levi Trumball, 24, committed suicide (see text).
- October 1985—Leominster, Massachusetts—John P. Finn, 15, committed suicide (see text).
- 4 October 1985—Slough, Berks, England—During the next two weeks, five teenage girls attempted suicide.
- November 1985–March 1986—Chicago's Northwest Side—Four teen suicides and eight attempts occurred.
- December 1985–December 1986—LaCrosse, Minnesota—Several teens committed suicide.
- 20 December 1985—Helena, Montana—The latest teen suicide was the eighteenth in Lewis and Clark County in 1985, and the second by a Capital High student. Four other teenagers who were former Capital students killed themselves in 1985. Since 1981, fifteen people aged 13–24 have killed themselves in the Helena area, and all were either students or former students at Capital High, one of two public high schools in Helena.
- 31 December 1985—Leominster, Massachusetts—William J. Lovetro, 17, committed suicide (see text).
- 11 January 1986—Mankato, Minnesota—Bryan Javens, 18, committed suicide (see text).
- 3 February 1986—Omaha, Nebraska—Michele M. Money, 16, committed suicide (see text).
- 4 February 1986—Omaha, Nebraska—Mark E. Walpus, 15, committed suicide (see text).
- 7 February 1986—Omaha, Nebraska—Thomas E. Wacha IV, 18, committed suicide. Four other teens made serious attempts on their lives during this same time period (see text).
- 10 February 1986—Spencer, Massachusetts—Francis V. McNamara, 16, committed suicide. In the next few days, eighteen other teens attempted to kill themselves (see text).
- 11 February 1986—Mankato, Minnesota—Diane Lamont, 15, committed suicide (see text).
- 18 February 1986—North Sioux City, South Dakota—Sandra Stephensen, 17, of rural Jefferson, South Dakota, and John Meier, 18, of Sioux City, Iowa, died in the closed garage at the Stephensen's home. The cause of death was listed as carbon

monoxide poisoning. Their deaths brought the number of suicides and murder-suicides in Union County, South Dakota, in one month to eight; most were farm-related.

- 19 February 1986—Mankato, Minnesota—Kimberly Evers, 20, committed suicide (see text).
- 23 February 1986—Plano, Texas—An 18-year-old committed suicide (see text).
- March 1986—Palos Heights, Illinois—The latest in a series of teen suicides to hit Shephard High School, near Chicago, occurred.
- 18 March 1986—Wind River, Wyoming—An 18-year-old youth committed suicide (see text).
- 22 March 1986—Fort Lauderdale, Florida—A 22-year-old sophomore from Western Illinois University became the fourth student to fall to his death from a local hotel during that season's spring break. Heavy drinking was said to be involved in two of the four incidents, and speculation as to the role of suicidal and self-destructive behavior was raised because of the deaths.
- 26 March 1986—Leominster, Massachusetts—George Henderson, 14, committed suicide. At least fifty youths have attempted suicide in the city in the last six months (see text).
- 8 April 1986—Japan—Recording star Yukiko Okada, 18, jumped from the roof of her recording studio. In the next month, at least thirty-four young people throughout Japan committed suicide (see text).
- 26 April 1986—Mankato, Minnesota—Tim Scheitel, 17, committed suicide (see text).
- 18 June 1986—Leominster, Massachusetts—Michael Dionne, 20, committed suicide (see text).
- August 1986—Westchester County, New York—A teen committed suicide (see text).
- September 1986—Leominster, Massachusetts—A teen committed suicide (see text).
- January 1987—Newton, Massachusetts—Three teens, all males, killed themselves during the last three weeks of the month; several area high school students attempted suicide.
- February 1987—Bethel, Alaska—Rumors circulated in a nearby Eskimo village of a teen suicide pact; eight youths killed themselves in recent months.
- February 1987—Broken Arrow, Oklahoma—Eight young people committed suicide in the past six months.

- 18 and 24 February 1987—Kansas City, Missouri—Two O'Hara High School seniors, both members of a Death and Dying class, separately died of carbon monoxide poisoning.
- 11 March 1987—Bergenfield, New Jersey—Four teens committed suicide together by carbon monoxide poisoning; four other youths' deaths since last June may have been suicide.
- 12 March 1987—Alsip, Illinois—Two teenage women died of carbon monoxide poisoning in apparent imitation of the New Jersey suicides.

Appendix Two: *The Deer Hunter*

DR. THOMAS RADECKI, psychiatrist at the University of Illinois School of Medicine, has been following the deaths allegedly caused by the showing of the movie, *The Deer Hunter*, for several years. Below is his list of known related suicides and other deaths.

- George Leonard Smith, 21, of Weatherford, Oklahoma, killed himself on 23 January 1978, imitating the Russian roulette scene from *The Deer Hunter* he had seen in a movie theater.
- Danny Turowski, 12, of Detroit, Michigan, died playing Russian roulette with his father's revolver at Lady Queen of Angels School, imitating a scene from *The Deer Hunter* (*Philadelphia Bulletin*-UPI, 5/11/79).
- Bruce K. Genke, 27, of St. Louis, Missouri, killed himself while reenacting *The Deer Hunter* in his car in the presence of a friend (*St. Louis Post-Dispatch*-UPI, 6/10/79).
- Dominick Didonato, 17, of Elizabeth, New Jersey, killed himself playing Russian roulette after having seen *The Deer Hunter* (9/3/79).
- A 16-year-old Helsinki, Finland, youth fatally shot himself play-

ing Russian roulette after seeing *The Deer Hunter* (Reuters, 1/18/80).

- Philip J. Hinshaw, 22, of Boulder, Colorado, killed himself acting out a scene from *The Deer Hunter* with a .38 caliber automatic in front of his cousin (*Rocky Mountain News*, 2/9/80). He died five months later.
- James R. Groeneveld, 16, of La Grange, Illinois, killed himself reenacting *The Deer Hunter* Russian roulette scene with a .38 caliber revolver belonging to his father (*San Francisco Examiner*-UPI, 3/21/80).
- Adolfo Flores Madrigal, 30, of Covina, California, killed himself while demonstrating Russian roulette with a .38 caliber revolver to two friends shortly after he had seen *The Deer Hunter*. He had drunk a few beers (*San Gabriel Valley Tribune*, 5/15/80).
- Timothy Wayne Grubbs, 21, of Midwest City, Oklahoma, killed himself with a .357 pistol shortly after watching *The Deer Hunter* on HBO cable TV. Grubbs was intoxicated at the time of playing the game (*Oklahoma City Times and Journal*, 5/25/80).
- Mickey Culpepper, 23, of Metairie, Louisiana, killed himself playing Russian roulette with a .38 caliber revolver, with a friend saying, "Look. I'm going to play *Deer Hunter*" (*New Orleans Times-Picayune*, 5/30/80).
- Timothy Rowe, 13, of Augusta, Georgia, killed himself with his aunt's .38 caliber revolver after watching *The Deer Hunter* on TV (*Atlanta Journal*, 6/16/80).
- Edward Eugene McClure, 17, of Indio, California, killed himself after watching *The Deer Hunter* on pay cable TV and playing Russian roulette with a .22 caliber revolver in front of his friends (*Coachella Valley Sun*, 5/29/80).
- John Phillip Triste, 8, of Mesa, Arizona, was killed by a 13-year-old friend with a .38 caliber revolver after his friend had watched *The Deer Hunter* on HBO cable TV (*Mesa Tribune*, 6/16/80).
- Robin Koontz, 26, of Ohioville, Pennsylvania, killed himself while discussing *The Deer Hunter* with friends and imitating the Russian roulette scene with a .357 magnum revolver (*Hartford Courant*-AP, 6/18/80).
- Richard Mendoza, 24, of San Antonio, Texas, killed himself while

still watching *The Deer Hunter* with a friend by shooting himself with a .22 caliber revolver saying, "I'm going to do it" (*Washington Post*, 10/15/80).

- An unidentified youth killed himself in the Philippines, playing Russian roulette in imitation of *The Deer Hunter*, according to the *San Francisco Examiner* (10/23/80).
- Anthony Totten, 16, committed suicide in San Ramon, California, with a .38 caliber revolver the day after watching *The Deer Hunter* on cable TV (*San Francisco Examiner*, 10/23/80).
- William R. Vinck, 21, of Elgin, South Carolina, killed himself playing Russian roulette with a revolver after watching *The Deer Hunter* (11/9/80).
- Mark Anderson, 19, of Jackson Township, New Jersey, killed himself playing Russian roulette one week after watching *The Deer Hunter* on TV. He was drinking whiskey with friends when he pulled out a revolver, spun the cylinder, placed the gun to his head, and fired. He was working for a cable TV station and in a good frame of mind earlier in the day (*Asbury Park Press*, 11/12/80). The program apparently was seen on WOR-TV, which had paid $400,000 for the rights to air the film.
- Godfrey Saganowski, Jr., 13, of Trenton, New Jersey, shot himself in the head while discussing *The Deer Hunter* with his brother. They had seen it the night before, apparently on WOR-TV (*Trenton Times*, 11/18/80).
- Brian Jackson, 28, an Army veteran of South Holland, Illinois, killed himself playing Russian roulette while demonstrating it to his brother, Craig, with a .357 caliber revolver. Jackson had bought a video tape of *The Deer Hunter* two weeks earlier. There was no history of psychological problems or depression (1/26/81 newspaper clipping).
- Joseph Avalos, 29, of San Antonio, Texas, killed himself playing *The Deer Hunter* with a revolver (2/5/81).
- Charles J. Koerth III, 15, of San Antonio, Texas, killed himself with a revolver playing Russian roulette after watching *The Deer Hunter* (2/6/81).
- John W. Dorko, 23, of Piscataway, New Jersey, killed himself with a .38 caliber revolver while playing Russian roulette with his cousin after they had seen *The Deer Hunter* on television (*The Review*, Edison, New Jersey, 2/19/81).
- Joseph Murray, 19, of Olney, Pennsylvania, killed himself with a

.38 caliber revolver playing Russian roulette with friends who has seen *The Deer Hunter* together the week before (*Philadelphia Inquirer*, 5/17/81).

- David Bouley, 23, of Andover, Minnesota, killed himself playing Russian roulette with a .38 caliber revolver at a party, while drinking the day after seeing *The Deer Hunter* on television. He shouted, "Want to play a game?" then spun the barrel, put the gun to his head, and pulled the trigger (UPI, 6/24/81).
- Bobby Joe Truelove, 22, of Oklahoma City, Oklahoma, died of a pistol bullet in his head after playing Russian roulette with a friend. He was inspired by *The Deer Hunter* (*Oklahoma City Times* 9/1/81).
- Matt Cianciulli III of Philadelphia, Pennsylvania, killed himself playing Russian roulette after watching *The Deer Hunter* (11/4/81).
- David Radnis, 28, of Woodridge, Illinois, shot himself in the head while seated at the kitchen table playing *Deer Hunter*, shortly after watching the movie on WFLD-TV in Chicago (*Chicago Tribune*, 11/24/81).
- Ted Tolwinski, 26, a tool-and-die maker, Chicago, Illinois, killed himself within two hours of seeing *The Deer Hunter* on WFLD-TV by playing Russian roulette in his kitchen in front of his wife with a gun he had just borrowed from a neighbor for that purpose. Tolwinski had been drinking and had first pointed the gun at his wife and pulled the trigger before pointing it at himself (*Chicago Tribune*, 11/24/81). NCTV had warned WFLD of the risks before the showing, and radio and newspaper coverage in Chicago opposed the showing. WFLD refused to debate NCTV on radio talk shows both before and after the deaths.
- Paul Whittaker, 17, of Denver, Colorado, killed himself with a .22 caliber revolver while playing Russian roulette with his brother and two girls the day after *The Deer Hunter* was shown on broadcast TV (KMGH-TV News clip, 1/20/82). Four other Russian roulette deaths occurred within six days of this, but newspaper reports do not mention whether the victims had seen the film (Nicholas Wendt, Aripeka, Florida, 1/14/82, *Lakeland Ledger*; Matthew Stone, Santa Clara, California, 1/14/82, *San Jose Mercury*; Lawrence Kelly, Deerfield Beach, Florida, 1/19/82, *Ft. Lauderdale News*; Alfonso Munoz, Bexar County, Texas, 1/24/82). The film was being shown widely around the country at this time.

- Bryan Petro, 14, of Indianapolis, Indiana, fatally shot himself in the head after watching *The Deer Hunter* on videotape at his father's TV store, and used his father's .38 caliber revolver (*Indianapolis News*, 12/23/82).
- Robert Call, 13, of Kansas City, Kansas, shot himself in the head with his father's .357 magnum at a friend's home, imitating *The Deer Hunter* (AP, 1/19/83).
- Christopher Mahan, 17, of Fairport, New York, killed himself playing Russian roulette in imitation of *The Deer Hunter* at a suburban high school party in his home while his parents were away. He had been drinking and had used his father's .38 revolver. The student had been very interested in violent movies and music videos and had been discussing these and *The Deer Hunter* before the shooting. His friends fled the scene without reporting it to the police (AP, 3/2/84).
- Steven R. McGill, 28, a prison guard in Providence, Rhode Island, has been arraigned for murder in the death of a prisoner whom he killed with a bullet in the head while he had been talking about *The Deer Hunter* and after unsuccessfully taunting other guards to play Russian roulette with him (*Providence Journal-Bulletin*, July 1984).
- Peter Richards, 14, of Trenton, New Jersey, killed himself with his father's revolver while playing Russian roulette (*Trentonian*, 2/23/85). He had watched *The Deer Hunter* on TV with his father, a police officer (reported by John Leahy of the *Trenton Monitor*).
- Andrea Scanzi, 14, of Como, Italy, killed himself on 15 April 1985 with a Magnum revolver after watching *The Deer Hunter* on broadcast TV (*Milan Corriere*, 4/16/85).

Serious, but Nonlethal Imitations

- Craig Miller, 17, of Tucson, Arizona, saw *The Deer Hunter* on HBO and was demonstrating Russian roulette to his girlfriend when he shot himself in the head with a .357 Magnum one hour before his Flowing Wells High School graduation. Craig gradually recovered over a 1½-year period (private letter).
- Stewart Robinson, 11, of Muncie, Indiana, shot himself in the head with his father's .38 caliber revolver during a game of Russian roulette with three playmates (*South Bend Tribune*, 7/9/80). Although in critical condition at first, the boy made a consid-

erable recovery and did appear on "CBS Morning News" two years later.

- John C. Williams, 25, in New York City, New York, was kidnapped near the World Trade Center. He was robbed, and the thieves tortured him playing Russian roulette, borrowing the torture technique from *The Deer Hunter* (*Baltimore Sun*, 10/8/80).
- An unidentified White House Secret Service agent shot himself in the head after playing Russian roulette when several agents watched the White House HBO showing of *The Deer Hunter*. Secret Service spokesman Jack Warner refused to confirm the details, but said that an agent was in a local hospital recovering from an accidental gunshot wound (*Washington Star*, 11/21/80).

In the January–March 1986 issue of Radecki's *National Coalition on Television Violence News*, the following update was published.

> Deerhunter Deaths Climb to 43: WGN-TV, Lebanon and Malaysia
>
> *Another death inspired by the Russian roulette scene in* The Deer Hunter *was reported in Dallas, Texas, where a 26-year-old man shot himself in the head while still watching the program on TV (*Dallas News, *8/31/85). The death parallels aggression research where the victims most often resemble the victim in the movie and where the strongest impact is immediately after viewing or even while still viewing. The movie had been shown on WGN Cable TV out of Chicago, which is owned by the Chicago* Tribune. *A death was predictable in view of the well-established connection between the airing of this film and imitation and the large number of viewers who receive WGN.*
>
> *NCTV received a report of two recent* Deer Hunter *deaths in Malaysia through our contacts with the International Coalition Against Violent Entertainment. Three other deaths were reported in the past year in* Newsweek *magazine from Lebanon where* The Deer Hunter *has set off a wave of young Lebanese now playing fatalistic games of Russian roulette. Numerous other cases of Russian roulette have been reported to NCTV, e.g. two in Miami occurring with thirty minutes of each other in widely separated parts of town.*

NCTV may be contacted at P.O. Box 2157, Champaign, Illinois 61820.

Appendix Three: Suicide Warning Signs

ACCORDING to most studies, eighty percent of all suicide victims give some kind of overt or coded message that they are planning or seriously thinking about killing themselves. A series of these signs should be taken as a cry for help:

- acts of aggression/violent behavior
- passive behavior
- running away
- alcohol and/or drug abuse
- changes in eating habits
- changes in sleeping behavior/insomnia
- frequent crying
- sudden changes in personality
- sudden mood swings
- impulsivity
- lack of interest in school work/decline in grades
- difficulty concentrating
- loss or lack of friends
- preoccupation with death
- decline in personal appearance

Right before a suicide, the following events may occur to set the stage for the final act:

- loss of an important person, animal, or thing
- an angry argument
- episodes of profound hopelessness
- threatening suicide
- making a will
- giving away prized possessions
- renewed perkiness (the suicidal decision has been made)
- making a suicidal plan/attempt

Obviously, human beings are complex, and not all people will demonstrate the same set of suicide warning signs. Nevertheless, the appearance of a series of these behaviors should call for some form of professional crisis intervention. And remember, on an individual basis, asking someone if he is thinking about killing himself does not put the idea in his head. It usually reassures a suicidal individual that you are not afraid to deal with him and what he is already considering, directly and openly.

For further information about suicide and suicide prevention, contact:

American Association of Suicidology
2459 South Ash
Denver, Colorado 80222
(303) 692-0985

For continuing updates on suicide cluster data and research, contact:

Loren Coleman, Research Associate
Center for Research and Advanced Study
University of Southern Maine
246 Deering Avenue
Portland, Maine 04102
(207) 780-4430

Appendix Four:
Teen Suicide Cluster Checklist

COMMUNITY leaders, police, parents, educators, adolescents, and others often want to know what specifics they should be aware of or do when a suicide cluster erupts. The following checklist issues from the experiences of many teen suicide clusters of the 1980s.

- Watch for a series of similar suicides in terms of age and sex of the individual victims, methods used, closeness in time, schools attended, peer groupings, and residences. If a pattern develops, you probably have a cluster in your community.
- Identify the close friends and associates of the cluster victims. Whether or not a true suicide pact exists, all of the intimates of the suicide are at high risk.
- Encourage, in a supportive fashion, the families of any teens who commit suicide to hold the sittings, wakes, and funerals on weekends. Teens should not be given the message they can stop the world if they kill themselves.
- Avoid holding large school assemblies and public address announcements about the latest suicide. There is evidence to

the effect that these actions tend to memorialize and romanticize the suicides, thus extending the problem. It is better to address the situation on a smaller scale, for example in a homeroom discussion.

- Involve all segments of the community, especially the local press, in downplaying the suicides. The reports of the suicides should not be sensationalized. Media blitzes about the suicides may backfire.
- Do create a crisis management team of all involved professionals, schoolwide or communitywide.
- Make available free *individual* counseling (versus group therapy) to those adolescents who ask for help or are identified as in need of intervention. Make available counseling for the families of these same youth and the families who have lost someone to suicide.
- Publicize your local crisis hotline number, and if you do not have one, pool community resources to create one. Teens use the telephone, will call a hotline to get help, and such an intervention could save a life.

References

Introduction

Binns, W., Kerkinan, D., and Schroeder, S. "Destructive Group Dynamics: An Account of Some Peculiar Interrelated Incidents of Suicide and Suicidal Attempts in a University Dormitory." *Journal of the American College Health Association* 14 (1966).

Centers for Disease Control. *Youth Suicide in the United States, 1970–1980.* Atlanta: CDC, 1980.

Hafen, Brent Q. and Frandsen, Kathryn J. *Youth Suicide.* Provo, UT: Behavioral Health Associates, 1986.

Handkoff, L. D. "An Epidemic of Attempted Suicide," *Comprehensive Psychiatry* 2 (1967).

Hendin, Herbert. *Suicide in America.* New York: W. W. Norton, 1982.

McIntosh, John L. *Research on Suicide: A Bibliography.* Westport, CT: Greenwood Press, 1985.

Meerloo, J. A. M. *Suicide and Mass Suicide.* New York: E. P. Dutton, 1962.

Peck, Michael L., Farberow, Norman L., and Litman, Robert E. *Youth Suicide.* New York: Springer, 1985.

Quinn, John C., ed. "Teen Suicides," *USA Today*, 27 February 1984.
Quinn, John C., ed. "Teen Suicide: Fall's Hot Made-for-TV Topic," *USA Today*, 27 August 1984.
Resnik, H. L. P. "The Neglected Search for the Suicidoccus Contagiosa," *Archives of Environmental Health*, 19 (September 1969).
Robbins, David and Conroy, Richard C. (1983). "A Cluster of Adolescent Suicide Attempts: Is Suicide Contagious?" *Journal of Adolescent Health Care* 3 (January 1983).
Rounsaville, Bruce J. and Weissman, Myrna M. "A Note on Suicidal Behaviors among Intimates," *Suicide and Life-Threatening Behavior*, 1:1 (Spring 1980).
Sieden, Richard. "The Youthful Suicide Epidemic," *Public Affairs Report*, 25 (1984).
Stewart, Sally Ann. "Did Andrew Chilstrom Have to Die?" *USA Today*, 6 February 1985.
"A Suicide Epidemic in a Psychiatric Hospital," *Diseases of the Nervous System* 38 (1977).
Tabachnick, Norman. "The Psychology of Fatal Accident," *Essays in Self-Destruction*. New York: Science House, 1967.
Theodorson, G. A. and Theodorson, A. G. *A Modern Dictionary of Sociology*. New York: Barnes and Noble/Harper & Row, 1979.
"2,500 Suicides Reported (in Nazi Poland)," *New York Times*, 23 January 1940.

PART 1

In Search of Ancient Clusters

Allen, N. "History and Background of Suicide," *Suicide: Assessment and Intervention*. New York: Appleton-Century-Crofts, 1977.
Alvarez, A. *The Savage God: A Study of Suicide*. New York: Random House, 1972.
Cavan, Ruth Shonle. *Suicide*. New York: Russell & Russell, 1965.
Choron, James. "Notes on Suicide Prevention in Antiquity," *Bulletin of Suicidology* 4 (July 1968).
Davis, Patricia A. *Suicidal Adolescents*. Springfield, IL: Charles C. Thomas, 1983.
Farberow, Norman L. "Cultural History of Suicide." *Suicide and*

Attempted Suicide. Stockholm: Nordiska Bokhandlens Forlag, 1972.

Garland, Robert. "Death Without Dishonour—Suicide in the Ancient World," *History Today* 33 (January 1983).

Gibbons, Edward. *The Decline and Fall of the Roman Empire.* New York: Harcourt, Brace, 1960.

Grosser, Halpern. *The Causes and Effects of Anti-Semitism.* New York: Philosophical Library, 1978.

Hankoff, L. D. *Suicide: Theory and Clinical Aspects.* Littleton, MA: PSG, 1979.

Hecker, J. F. C. *Epidemics of the Middle Ages.* London: Trubner, 1859.

"Josce of York," "Yom Tov of Joigny," and "York." *Encyclopedia Judia.* New York: Macmillan, 1971.

Leftowitz, Mary R. and Fant, Maureen B. *Women in Greece and Rome.* Toronto: Samuel-Stevens, 1977.

Meerloo, op. cit.

Morrow, Lance. "The Lure of Doomsday," *Time,* 112:23, 4 December 1978.

O'Dea, James J. *Suicide: Studies on its Philosophy, Causes, and Prevention.* New York: G. P. Putnam's, 1882.

Valente, M. "History of Suicide," *Suicide: Assessment and Intervention.* Norwalk, CT: Appleton-Century-Crofts, 1984.

Whitson, W., trans. *The Works of Flavius Josephus.* New York: World Publishing House, 1875.

Islands of Clusters

Alabastro, Ruben G. "Mass Suicide in the Philippines," Associated Press. 19 September 1985.

Alexander, W. J. Wage Labor, Urbanization, and Culture Change in the Marshall Islands: The Ebeye Case. Ph.D. Dissertation, New School for Social Research (1978).

Alvarez, op. cit.

Burgess, John. "Seven Japanese Women Kill Selves After Cult Leader Dies," Huntsville (Alabama) *Times,* 3 November 1986.

Dwyer, Philip M. "An Inquiry into the Psychological Dimensions of Cult Suicide," *Suicide and Life-Threatening Behavior,* 9:2 (Summer 1979).

Hall, John R. "Apocalypse at Jonestown," *Society,* 16:6 (1979).

Matthews, Tom, et al. "The Cult of Death," *Newsweek*, 112:23, 4 December 1978.
Morrow, op. cit.
Neff, Donald. "Nightmare in Jonestown," *Time*, 112:23, 4 December 1978.
O'Neill, Richard. *Suicide Squads*. New York: Ballantine, 1984.
Patterson, Carolyn Bennett. "In the Far Pacific: At the Birth of Nations," *National Geographic*, 170:4 (October 1986).
Rubinstein, Donald H. "Epidemic Suicide Among Micronesian Adolescents," *Social Science and Medicine*, 17:10 (1983).
Stack, Steven. "The Effect of the Jonestown Suicides on American Suicide Rates," *Journal of Social Psychology*, 119 (1983).
"Suicide, Emigrations Plague Western Samoa," Portland, ME: *Press-Herald*, 17 September 1986.
Woodward, Kenneth L., *et al*. "How They Bend Minds," *Newsweek*, 112:23, 4 December 1978.

Fiery Clusters

"Another Suicide Arouses Vietnam," *New York Times*, 5 August 1963.
Ashton, John R. and Donnan, Stuart. "Suicide by Burning as an Epidemic Phenomenon: An Analysis of 82 Deaths and Inquests in England and Wales in 1978–9," *Psychological Medicine*, 11 (1981).
Buckley, Thomas. "Man, 22, Immolates Himself in Antiwar Protest at U.N.," *New York Times*, 10 November 1965.
"Burned Student Still in Danger," *New York Times*, 26 December 1974.
"Cripple a Suicide by Fire in Queens," *New York Times*, 14 August 1970.
Crosby, K., Rhee, J., and Holland, J. "Suicide by Fire: A Contemporary Method of Political Protest," *International Journal of Social Psychiatry*, 23 (1977).
Halberstam, David. "Nun's Act a Surprise," *New York Times*, 16 August 1963.
Hess, John L. "France Stirred by Immolations," *New York Times*, 25 January 1970.
Jones, David. "Woman, 82, Sets Herself Afire in Street as Protest on Vietnam," *New York Times*, 18 March 1965.

"Monk Suicide by Fire in Anti-Diem Protest," *New York Times*, 11 June 1963.
"Montclair Student Sets Himself Afire," *New York Times*, 24 December 1974.
"Mother Attempts Suicide by Burning," *New York Times*, 12 November 1965.
"Motorist Suicide by Fire," *New York Times*, 17 July 1969.
"Rebel in Torch Horror (in Korea)," *London Sun*, 23 May 1986.
"Requiem Tomorrow for Pacifist Suicide," *New York Times*, 12 November 1965.
"Seton Hall Student Kills Self by Fire," *New York Times*, 6 October 1970.
Severo, Richard. "Man Immolates Himself in Times Sq." *New York Times*, 19 July 1970.
Shuster, Alvin. "Czech Immolates Himself by Fire," *New York Times*, 17 January 1969.
Shuster, Alvin. "Czech Protester Dies of His Burns," *New York Times*, 20 January 1969.
"Suicide at Bear Mountain," *New York Times*, 8 December 1974.
"Times Square Suicide Was Ex-N.Y.U. Student," *New York Times*, 20 July 1970.
"2 More Buddhists Suicides by Burning in Vietnam Protest," *New York Times*, 16 August 1963.
"2 More French Fire Suicides," *New York Times*, 31 January 1970.
"2 More Persons in France Commit Suicide by Fire," *New York Times*, 27 January 1970.
"Two Women Set Afire," *New York Times*, 11 November 1972.
"Veteran in Danang Dies in Immolation by Fire," *New York Times*, 25 August 1971.
"Wisconsin Student Burned," *New York Times*, 19 February 1972.
"Woman in Moscow Sets Herself Afire," *New York Times*, 10 March 1974.
"Woman a Suicide by Fire," *New York Times*, 29 August 1972.
"Youth's Immolation Said to Stir Rioting in a Lithuanian City," *New York Times*, 22 May 1972.

Clusters of a Stressful Age

Agence France-Press. "A Baffling Series of Suicides," *San Francisco Chronicle*, 12 April 1974.

"AIDS May Have Caused Suicide Pact," *Calgary Herald*, 25 October 1986.

Bohuslawsky, Maria. "Poor Farm Economy Linked to Suicide Rate," *Winnipeg Free Press*, 3 February 1986.

" 'Burnout' Spurs Farmer's Frenzy," *Boston Herald*, 29 April 1986.

Cope, Lewis. "Minnesota, 5 States Plan Joint Study of Farm Suicides," *Minneapolis Star and Tribune*, 5 March 1986.

DeVore, Brian. "2 Teen-Agers Commit Suicide," *Des Moines Register*, 20 February 1986.

"Farm Saved by $187,000 from Donors," *USA Today*, 23 December 1986.

"Farm Wife Kills Self Over Family's Financial Problems," Associated Press, 11 July 1986.

Gibson, Paul. "Gay Male and Lesbian Youth Suicide." Presented at Oakland, CA: National Conference on Prevention and Intervention in Youth Suicide, 11 June 1986.

Goldblum, Peter and Moulton, Jeffrey. "AIDS-Related Suicide: A Dilemma for Health Care Providers," *FOCUS*/University of California at San Francisco, 2:1 (November 1986).

Gutis, Philip S. "Officer's Suicide Reflects Pressures on Suffolk Police," *New York Times*, 16 January 1987.

Hartman, Curtis. "On the Road: Johnson County, Iowa—An American Tragedy," *Inc.* (May 1986).

Loo, Robert. "Suicide Among Police in a Federal Force," *Suicide and Life-Threatening Behavior*, 16:3 (Fall 1986).

"Man Who Lost Farm at Auction Slays His Family, Sets House Afire, Kills Self," Associated Press, 22 August 1986.

Miller, Kay. "An Iowa Farmer's Day of Death," *Minneapolis Star and Tribune Sunday Magazine*, 23 February 1986.

Nix, Crystal. "Police Suicide: Answers are Sought," *New York Times*, 15 September 1986.

"N.Y. Officer Kills Self After Arrest," Associated Press, 9 September 1986.

Poirier, Patricia. "Mounties Cite Suicide Rate in Drive to Obtain Union," *Toronto Globe and Mail*, 30 September 1986.

"Police Detective Suicide Victim at Suffolk Downs," Woonsocket, RI: *Call*, 24 May 1986.

Rofes, Eric E. *"I Thought People Like That Killed Themselves": Lesbians, Gay Men and Suicide*. San Francisco: Grey Fox Press, 1983.

Shilts, Randy. "Suicidal AIDS Victim Saved," *San Francisco Chronicle*, 8 May 1985.
"Soldier Tested for AIDS Commits Suicide," *Equal Time*, 19 February 1986.
"Suicidal Man Chased by Police," United Press International, 28 April 1986.
Swartzburg, Marshall. "Dual Suicides in Homosexuals," *Journal of Nervous and Mental Disorder*, 155:2 (1972).
'Three Police Deaths 'Tragic Coincidence,' " Attleboro, MA: *Sun Chronicle*, 19 April 1986.
"Toronto Police Officer Commits Suicide," *Calgary Herald*, 16 November 1986.
"2 Hub Policemen Shoot Selves Fatally," Worcester, MA: *Telegram*, 18 April 1986.
"Union County's Latest Suicides," United Press International, 20 February 1986.

The Spurious, Curious and Dubious

Amory, Cleveland. "After Living With Man, A Dolphin May Commit Suicide," *Holiday*. (1970).
"Astronomer Links Comet to Floods," Portland, ME: *Press-Herald*, 5 February 1986.
Burnam, Tom. *More Misinformation*. New York: Ballantine, 1980.
Calder, Nigel. *The Comet Is Coming!* New York: Viking, 1980.
Chapman, Robert D. and Brandt, John C. *The Comet Book*. Boston: Jones and Bartlett, 1984.
Clube, Victor and Napier, Bill. *The Cosmic Serpent*. London: Faber and Faber, 1982.
Coleman, Loren. "Comets and Suicides: Astrosociological Folklore?" *Fortean Times*, 47 (Autumn 1986).
Doherty, Paul B. *The Arrival of Halley's Comet*. Woodbury, NY: Barron's, 1985.
Flaste, Richard, *et al*. *The New York Times Guide to the Return of Halley's Comet*. New York: Times Books, 1985.
Freud, Sigmund. "Zur Selbstmond Diskussion," *Diskussion des Weiner Psychoanalytischen Vereins*, 1910.
Fuller, Mary Margaret, ed. "Suicidal Reaction," *Fate*, 39:8 (August 1986).
Gallant, Roy. Personal communication. (1986).

Gillette, William. Personal communication. (1986).
Goodavage, Joseph F. *The Comet Kohoutek*. New York: Pinnacle, 1973.
Gropman, Donald with Mirvus, Kenneth. *Comet Fever*. New York: Fireside/Simon & Schuster, 1985.
Hart, Matthew. *A Viewer's Guide to Halley's Comet*. New York: Pocket, 1985.
Hecker, J. F. C. *Epidemics of the Middle Ages*. London: Trubner, 1859.
"Killed Watching for Comet," *New York Times*, 19 May 1910.
Marquis, Thomas P. *Keep the Last Bullet for Yourself*. New York: Reference Publications, 1976.
May, John. *Curious Facts*. New York: Holt, Rinehart and Winston, 1980.
Metz, Jerred. *Halley's Comet, 1910: Fire in the Sky*. St. Louis: Singing Bone Press, 1985.
Moore, Patrick. *Comets*. New York: Scribners, 1986.
National Conference on Youth Suicide. Washington, D.C., 19–20 June 1985.
Olson, Roberta J. M. *Fire and Ice: A History of Comets in Art*. New York: Walker, 1985.
"1,050 Alpine Sheep Commit Mass Suicide," *Toronto Star*, 26 July 1970.
Rickard, Robert J. M. "Diary of a Mad Planet: The 1985–86 Visit of Halley's Comet," *Fortean Times*, 47 (Autumn 1986).
Ritchie, David. *Comets: The Swords of Heaven*. New York: Signet, 1985.
Sagan, Carl and Druyan, Ann. *Comet*. New York: Random House, 1985.
Sanderson, Ivan T. *Living Mammals of the World*. Garden City, NY: Hanover House, 1956.
Scott, Douglas D. Personal communication. (1986).
Scott, Douglas D. and Connor, Melissa A. "Post-mortem at the Little Bighorn," *Natural History*, 95:6 (June 1986).
"Some Driven to Suicide," *New York Times*, 19 May 1910.
Spencer, Jerry D. "George Custer and the Battle of the Little Bighorn: Homicide or Mass Suicide?" *Journal of Forensic Science*, 28 (1983).
Starr, Douglas. "Whale Suicides," *Omni*, 8:10 (July 1986).
Taylor, Charles S. "Comets—Are They Linked to Suicides?" Minden, LA: *Press-Herald*, 7 April 1986.

Wells, James. "Suicide in Children and Adolescents," presented at Portland, ME: Northeast Regional Child Welfare League of America Conference, 12 June 1985.

Whipple, Fred L. *The Mystery of Comets.* Washington, D.C.: Smithsonian, 1985.

PART 2

Today's Epidemic of Youth Suicide Clusters

Bollen, Kenneth A. "Temporal Variations in Mortality," *Demography*, 20:1 (February 1983).

Cohen, Susan and Daniel. *Teenage Stress.* New York: M. Evans, 1984.

Dublin, Louis I. *Suicide: A Sociological and Statistical Study.* New York: Ronald, 1963.

Kevan, Simon M. *Perspectives on Season of Suicide.* London: Pergamon, 1980.

Kunz, Phillip R. "Relationship Between Suicide and Month of Birth," *Psychological Reports*, 42 (1978).

Lester, David and Beck, Aaron T. "Suicide and National Holidays," *Psychological Reports*, 36 (1975).

Phillips, David P. and Liu, Judith. "The Frequency of Suicides Around Major Holidays: Some Surprising Findings," *Suicide and Life-Threatening Behavior*, 10:1 (Spring 1980).

"Teen Suicides: Is There a Pattern?" *Science News*, 31 March 1984.

Boomtown Pressures and the Texas Clusters

Gelman, David and Gangelhoff, B. K. "Teen-age Suicide in the Sun Belt," *Time*, 15 August 1983.

Herbaugh, Sharon. "Suicides," Portland, ME: *Press-Herald*, 17 October 1984.

"Houston Suburb Institutes Anti-Suicide Plan," *New York Times*, 14 October 1984.

Lehr, Dick. "Teen-age Suicides: How One City Coped," *Boston Globe*, 29 March 1985.

"Number of Teen-Age Suicides Alarms Parents in Texas City," *New York Times*, 4 September 1983.

Quinn, John, ed. "4th Houston-area Youth Kills Self Since Saturday," *USA Today*, 12 October 1984.
"Teen-Age Suicides Stir Texas Prevention Drive," *New York Times*, 12 April 1984.
"Youth Kills Himself Over Broken Romance," *New York Times*, 25 August 1983.

Death in Suburbia

"Boy, 14, Is Found Hanged on Tree," *New York Times*, 16 February 1984.
Brody, Jane E. "The Haunting Specter of Teen-Age Suicide," *New York Times*, 4 March 1984.
"Death of Girl, 15, Ruled a Suicide," *New York Times*, 22 September 1984.
"Foul Play Rejected in Student's Death," *New York Times*, 27 February 1984.
Frankel, Bruce and Johnson, Peter. "N.Y. Counties Stress Prevention in Response to Teen-age Suicides," *USA Today*, 3 November 1984.
"Girl, 15, Burns to Death on L.I.," *New York Times*, 5 October 1984.
"Girl Shot to Death; Suicide Suspected," *New York Times*, 14 September 1984.
Keel, John A. Personal communication. (1986).
Kriss, Gary. "County Stressing Suicide Programs," *New York Times*, 4 March 1984.
McGill, Douglas C. "Fordham Student Hangs Himself at Parent's Home in Westchester," *New York Times*, 26 February 1984.
"Mother Finds Boy Hanged in Attic," *New York Times*, 18 October 1984.
"Putnam Man, 21, Is Found Hanged," *New York Times*, 24 December 1984.
Spoonhour, Anne. "The First Few Days Are The Hardest," *People*, 23:7 (18 February 1985).
"Suicide Suspected in Youth's Death," *New York Times*, 22 December 1984.
"Team to Examine Teen-Age Suicides," *New York Times*, 19 March 1984.
Treaster, Joseph B. "Another Teen-Ager Is Believed a Suicide in Westchester Area," *New York Times*, 16 March 1984.

Walden, Geoff. "Dad Blames Son's Death on TV Movie," *Gannett Westchester Newspaper*, 21 February 1985.

"Westchester Man, 20, Is Found Dead in Yard," *New York Times*, 30 July 1984.

Williams, Lena. "Fourth Teen-Ager's Suicide Shocks 2 Suburban Counties," *New York Times*, 23 February 1984.

Williams, Lena. "The Life and Death of Justin, 14," *New York Times*, 14 March 1984.

Williams, Lena. "A Youth's Suicide Upstate Brings 200 People Together to Ask Why," *New York Times*, 18 February 1984.

"Youth's Death Ruled Suicide," Portland, ME: *Press-Herald*, 20 February 1985.

Goodbye Cruel World

"Anti-Suicide Efforts Stirring Resistance," Athol, MA: *Daily News*, 14 April 1986.

Boucher, Norman. "Why Here?" *Boston Sunday Globe Magazine*, 2 August 1986.

"CDC Official Not Concerned With Media Coverage," United Press International, 9 May 1986.

"Counselor Cited For Work Following Six Suicides," Athol, MA: *Daily News*, 6 June 1986.

Della Valle, Paul. "Leominster Leaders Unite on Youth's Problems," Worcester, MA: *Telegram*, 23 April 1986.

Lehr, Dick op. cit.

"Leominster Moment of Silence," United Press International, 27 March 1986.

MacLaughlin, Jim. "Another Teen Death Shocks Town," *Boston Herald*, 28 March 1986.

Malinowski, W. Zachary. "Rash of Suicides Puzzles Parents in Leominster," Providence, RI: *Sunday Journal*, 25 May 1986.

"Man's Death Ruled Suicide in Leominster," *Boston Globe*, 19 June 1986.

"6th Teen Suicide in Mass. Town," Associated Press, 27 March 1986.

"Town Has Rash of Teen Suicides," Associated Press, 4 November 1985.

"Town Stunned by Deaths of Teen-Age Girls," Associated Press, 4 November 1984.

Tri-Link, Inc. Personal communication. (1987).

Native American Clusters

"Arapahoe Youth's Hanging Added to Suicide Toll," Associated Press, 20 March 1986.

"8 Indian Suicides Stir Action," Associated Press, 29 September 1985.

Ensslin, John C. "Indian Reservation Copes with Epidemic of Suicides," Scripps Howard News Service, 7 October 1985.

"Indian Elders Fight Teen Suicide," Associated Press, 27 December 1985.

"Indian Suicide Rate Worst," *Toronto Sun*, 23 May 1986.

Miller, M. "Suicides on a Southwestern American Indian Reservation," *White Cloud Journal*, 1:3 (1979).

"9th Indian Commits Suicide," *USA Today*, 2 October 1985.

"Officials Meet on Indian Suicides," *Boston Globe*, 3 October 1985.

O'Gara, Geoffrey. "Teen Suicides Baffle Indian Tribes," *USA Today*, 1 October 1985.

"Puzzle of Nine Indian Suicides," United Press International, 1 October 1985.

"Reason for Suicides by Indians Disputed," *New York Times*, 2 April 1980.

Shore, James. Personal communication. (1985).

Short, Father Tony. Personal communication. (1985).

"String of Suicides Halted," *USA Today*, 4 November 1985.

"Suicide Crisis on Indian Reservation," *New York Times*, 30 September 1985.

Ward, J. A. and Fox, Joseph. "A Suicide Epidemic on An Indian Reserve," *Canadian Psychiatric Association Journal*, 22:8 (December 1977).

"Wind River's Lost Generation," *Time*, 31 October 1985.

A Week in February

"But for the Grace of God . . ." *U.S. News and World Report*, 24 February 1986.

"Depression Over Suicides Lifting," United Press International, 11 February 1986.

Devlin, Kevin. "Suicide Pact Theory on Shotgun Death of Youths," Belfast, Ireland: *Telegram*, 7 February 1986.

Dugan, Kevin. "Teen Suicides Start Preventative Campaign," United Press International News Service, 9 February 1986.

"Frustration Vented at Meetings," United Press International, 11 February 1986.

"Grieving Students Rally Against Suicides," United Press International, 10 February 1986.

Juffer, Jane and Weller, Tim. "Teen Deaths 'Affect Psyche' of Omaha," *USA Today*, 11 February 1986.

Prescod, Suzanne, ed. "Omaha Reacts to Rash of Recent Teen Suicides," Children & Teens Today, 6:8, April 1986.

Robbins, William. "3d Suicide Stuns Students in Omaha," *New York Times*, 11 February 1986.

"School Battles Suicide Threat," Associated Press, 10 February 1986.

"School Talks Over Suicide Wave," Associated Press, 11 February 1986.

"Students at High School Hit by 3 Suicides Urged to 'Choose Life,' Comfort Classmates," *Boston Globe*, 11 February 1986.

"Students Rally," United Press International, 13 February 1986.

"Three Suicides Last Week Shatter School," Portland, ME: *Press-Herald*, 10 February 1986.

"TV Station Helps to Avert Possible Suicide," United Press International, 12 February 1986.

In the Wake of Omaha?

Dietz, Jean. "Psychologist: Counseling Can Help Halt Suicides," *Boston Globe*, 14 February 1986.

Kaull, Mary. "Teen Suicide: Many Links in Deadly Chain," *USA Today*, 13 February 1986.

Nolan, Pat. Personal communication. (1986).

"Officials Discuss Suicides," United Press International, 12 February 1986.

"Parents Advised on Suicide," Associated Press, 13 February 1986.

"Parents Upset Over Media Coverage," United Press International, 14 February 1986.

"Parents Warned of Suicide 'Clusters,'" Associated Press, 14 February 1986.

Smock, Frederick A. "Group Forms in Wake of Suicide," Worcester, MA: *Telegram*, 22 April 1986.

"Suicide and Attempts Hit Town," Associated Press, 12 February 1986.

Witcher, Gregory. "Spencer Wondering in Wake of Teen-ager's Suicide," *Boston Globe*, 14 February 1986.

The 11th of the Month Club

Adams, Jim. "Latest Suicide Underscores Teen-Ager's Advice," *Minneapolis Star and Tribune*, 22 April 1986.

"Arden Hills Teen Suicide," United Press International, 21 April 1986.

"Copycat Suicide Rumor Stops Broadcast," Portland, ME: *Press-Herald*, 28 February 1986.

deFiebre, Conrad. "Teen's Suicide Is Fourth in Mankato in 3½ Months," *Minneapolis Star and Tribune*, 30 April 1986.

DeVore, Brain. "2 Teen-Agers Commit Suicide," *Des Moines Register*, 20 February 1986.

Galde, Phyllis. Personal communication. (1986).

Hall, Mark A. Personal communication. (1986).

"Mankato School Has Fourth Suicide," *Minneapolis Star and Tribune*, 27 November 1986.

"Mankato Youth Commits Suicide," *Mankato Free Press*, 28 April 1986.

Monsour, Theresa. "Focus Is on Suicide This Week," *St. Paul Pioneer Press and Dispatch*, 29 April 1986.

PART 3

Conclusions of the Cluster Investigators

Boucher, Norman. "Why Here?" *Boston Sunday Globe Magazine*, 2 August 1986.

"CDC Official Not Concerned with Media Coverage," United Press International, 9 May 1986.

Davidson, Jean. "Epidemic of Teenage Suicides Has Experts Searching for Cure," *Chicago Tribune*, 1 June 1986.

Davidson, Lucy. "Contagion and Media," presented at Department of Health and Human Services Task Force on Youth Suicide (May 1986).

Dietz, Jean. "Psychologist: Counseling Can Help Halt Suicides," *Boston Globe*, 14 February 1986.

Doan, Michael and Peterson, Sarah. "As Cluster Suicides Take Toll of Teenagers," *U.S. News and World Report*, 12 November 1984.

Gould, Madelyn. "Risk Factors for Suicide Contagion," presented at the Annual Meeting of the American Association of Suicidology, 3 April 1986.

Juffer, Jane and Weller, Tim. "Teen Deaths 'Affect Psyche' of Omaha," *USA Today*, 11 February 1986.

Kaull, Mary, "Teen Suicide: Many Links in Deadly Chain," *USA Today*, 13 February 1986.

Lehr, Dick. "Teen-age Suicides: How One City Coped," *Boston Globe*, 29 March 1985.

Malinowski, W. Zachary. "Rash of Suicides Puzzles Parents in Leominster," Providence, RI: *Sunday Journal*, 25 May 1986.

"Psychiatrist Fears Murder-Suicide Link," *Calgary Herald*, 22 September 1986.

Rosenberg, Mark. "Cluster Suicides," presented at the National Conference on Youth Suicide, 19 June 1985.

Taylor, Paul. "Cluster Phenomenon of Young Suicides Raises 'Contagion' Theory," *Washington Post*, 11 March 1984.

Tugend, Alina. "Suicide's 'Unanswerable Logic,' " *Education Week*, 18 June 1986.

Witcher, Gregory. "Spencer Wondering in Wake of Teen-ager's Suicide," *Boston Globe*, 14 February 1986.

The Media and Contagion

"Aircraft Crashes Nationwide Kill 19," Associated Press, 19 May 1986.

Baker, Sherry. "A Plague Called Violence," *Omni*, 8:11, August 1986.

Barraclough, B. M., Shephard, D., and Jennings, C. "Do Newspaper Reports of Coroners' Inquests Incite People to Commit Suicide?" *British Journal of Psychiatry* 131 (1977).

Berman, Alan L. "Mass Media and Youth Suicide Prevention," presented at the National Conference on Prevention and Interventions, Oakland, CA, 11 June 1986.

Bollen, Kenneth A. and Phillips, David P. "Imitative Suicides: A National Study of the Effects of Television News Stories," *American Sociological Review* 47 (December 1982).

Bollen, Kenneth A. and Phillips, David P. "Suicidal Motor Vehicle Fatalities in Detroit: A Replication," *American Journal of Sociology* 87 (1981).

Boorstin, Robert O. "Gunman at Midtown Office Kills 2 and Shoots Himself," *New York Times*, 17 May 1986.

Coleman, Loren. "Teen Suicide Clusters and the Werther Effect," University of Southern Maine: The *Network News* 3 (March 1986).

Eisenberg, Leon. "Does Bad News About Suicide Beget Bad News?" *New England Journal of Medicine* 315:11, 11 September 1986.

" 'Exorcist' Suicide," *San Francisco Chronicle*, 18 October 1986.

"Ex-Policeman, Wife Die in Hostage-Taking," Associated Press, 17 May 1986.

Gould, Madelyn S. and Shaffer, David. "The Impact of Suicide in Television Movies: Evidence of Imitation," *New England Journal of Medicine* 315:11, 11 September 1986.

Huntley, S. and Kennedy, H. "Expert Advice: Keep Control of Family Fun," *U.S. News and World Report*, 28 October 1985.

Hutchings, David. " 'I Started Thinking About Dying,' " *People*, 23:7, 18 February 1985.

"Mass Killer Commits Suicide," United Press International, 19 May 1986.

McEntee, Peg. "Wyoming Bombing Planned a Year Ahead," Associated Press (1986).

"Minnesota Man, 23, Kills Himself Trying Russian Roulette at Party," *New York Times*, 25 June 1981.

Motto, Jerome A. "Newspaper Influences on Suicide," *Archives of General Psychiatry* 23 (August 1970).

Ostroff, Robert B., *et al.* "Adolescent Suicides Modeled After Television Movie," *American Journal of Psychiatry* 142 (August 1985).

Phillips, David P. "Airplane Accident Fatalities Increase Just After Newspaper Stories About Suicide and Murder," *Science* 201 (25 August 1978).

Phillips, David P. "Airplane Accidents, Murder, and the Mass Media: Towards a Theory of Imitation and Suggestions," *Social Forces* 58:4 (June 1980).

Phillips, David P. "The Impact of Fictional Television Stories on U.S. Adult Fatalities: New Evidence on the Effect of the Mass Media on Violence," *American Journal of Sociology* 87:6 (1982).

Phillips, David P. "The Influence of Suggestion on Suicide: Substantive and Theoretical Implications of the Werther Effect," *American Sociological Review* 39:3 (June 1974).

Phillips, David P. "Media Attentions Helps Encourage Teen Suicide," *USA Today*, 19 September 1986.

Phillips, David P. "Motor Vehicle Fatalities Increase Just After Publicized Suicide Stories," *Science* 196 (24 June 1977).

Phillips, David P. "Suicide, Motor Vehicle Fatalities, and the Mass Media: Evidence Toward a Theory of Suggestion," *American Journal of Sociology* 84:5 (1979).

Phillips, David P. and Carstensen, Lundie L. "Clustering of Teenage Suicides After Television News Stories About Suicide," *New England Journal of Medicine* 315:11, 11 September 1986.

Radecki, Thomas. "Deer Hunter Deaths Climb to 43," *National Coalition on Television Violence News*, 7:1–2 (January–March 1986).

"Russian Roulette Fatal for Boy," *New York Times*, 25 October 1983.

Shepherd, Daphne and Barraclough, B. M. "Suicide Reporting: Information or Entertainment?" *British Journal of Psychiatry* 132 (1978).

Tugend, Alina, op. cit.

"TV Soap Opera Suicide Try Upsets Hospital," *Washington Post*, 9 June 1986.

"2 Die in Fiery Plane Crash on Atlantic City Road," *New York Times*, 19 May 1986.

"Two Die After Plea Fails to Halt Showing of Film," *New York Times*, 25 November 1981.

"2 Found Dead in Car in Bronx; Murder-Suicide Is Suspected," *New York Times*, 19 May 1986.

Walden, Geoff, op. cit.

Wilson, Jeff. "Marilyn Monroe: She Would Have Been 60 Today," Nashua, NH: *Telegraph*, 2 June 1986.

Music, the Message, and Suicide

Attig, Thomas. "Death Themes in Adolescent Music: The Classic Years." *Adolescence and Death*. New York: Springer (1986).

Corliss, Richard. "Sid and Nancy," *Time*, 3 November 1986.

"Did Song Lead to Teen Suicide," Associated Press, 14 January 1986.

Gewertz, Catherine. "Osbourne Suited Over Suicide," United Press International, 13 January 1986.

"Idol Leads Teens to Their Deaths," United Press International, 23 April 1986.
"Judge Dismisses Suit," United Press International, 8 August 1986.
Makihara, Kumiko. "Teen Deaths Wrack Japan," Associated Press, 24 April 1986.
Marsh, Dave. *Rock Book of Lists.* San Francisco: Rolling Stone (1982).
McGill, Peter. "Japan Upset at Copycat Suicides After Death of Pop Pop Star," *London Observer*, 21 April 1986.
Mitchell, Justin. "Rock Music as a Therapy Tool," Scripps Howard, 11 March 1986.
"Ozzy Osbourne Defends His Song," Associated Press, 23 January 1986.
"Parents Say Singer's Lyric Prompted Son's Suicide," Associated Press, 15 January 1986.
Robbins, D. and Conroy, R. C. "A Cluster of Adolescent Suicide Attempts: Is Suicide Contagious?" *Journal of Adolescent Health Care* 3 (1983).
Synder, Jane. "Wave of Suicides Rocks Japan," United Press International, 22 April 1986.
"Suit Against Osbourne Suicide Song Dismissed," Associated Press, 8 August 1986.
Wetherall, William. "Japanese Youth and the Yukiko Syndrome," *Far Eastern Economic Review*, 17 July 1986.
"Youth Suicide Wave in Japan," Associated Press, 22 April 1986.

Future Note

Durkheim, Emile, ed., John Spaulding and George Simpson, trans. *Suicide.* New York: Free Press (1981).
Henegar, Charles. Personal communication. (1986).

Teen Suicide Clusters of the 1980s: A Chronology

Davidson, Jean. "Epidemic of Teenage Suicides Has Experts Searching for Cure," *Chicago Tribune*, 1 June 1986.
Doan, Michael and Peterson, Sarah. "As Cluster Suicides Take Toll of Teenagers," *U.S. News and World Report*, 12 November 1984.
"Fourth Student Falls to Death," *Huntsville Times*, 23 March 1986.

Jordan, Mary. "Teen-Age Suicides Reduced by Fairfax Program, Hill Told," *Washington Post*, 4 October 1984.

"Montana Kids: Help Us Combat Suicides," Bismarck Tribune, 3 January 1986.

"New Bedford Police Close Book on Teen's Suicide," *Boston Herald*, 18 March 1986.

Quinn, John, ed. "Teen Suicide," *USA Today*, 26 February 1985.

Sciacca, Joe and Murphy, Shelley. "Probers Seek Answers to Tragic Triple Suicides," *Boston Herald*, 16 March 1985.

Taylor, Paul. "Cluster Phenomenon of Young Suicides Raises 'Contagion' Theory," *Washington Post*, 11 March 1984.

Tugend, Alina. "Suicide's 'Unanswerable Logic,' " *Education Week*, 18 June 1986.

About the Author

Loren Coleman M.S.W. has been directly involved in the social sciences since 1967 when he was an anthropology undergraduate and began working with youth and their families. He is the director of a two-year teen suicide project funded by the U.S. Department of Health and Human Services and a member of the American Association of Suicidology. Loren Coleman is a research associate at the Human Services Development Institute, Center for Research and Advanced Study, University of Southern Maine, and a sociology doctoral student in the Department of Sociology and Anthropology, University of New Hampshire. He is the author of four other books, including *Mysterious America* and *Curious Encounters*, both published by Faber and Faber. He lives with his wife, Libbet Cone, and son, Malcolm, in Portland, Maine.